# COWBOY ODYSSEY

# Cowboy Odyssey

**Terry Whistler**

Terry Whistler, Publisher
2014

First Printing: 2014

ISBN 978-1-312-73005-2

Terry Whistler
26015 Orleans
Tomball, TX 77377

www.terry.whistler@sbcglobal.net

# Dedication

*To a dear departed saint, my Aunt Zena (1909-2006),*
*an author in the making for most of her life,*
*who never got to see the dream of her novel*
*come true.*

# Contents

# Preface

It is said that art is difficult, but criticism is easy. Writing doesn't fare much better. It's difficult in a different kind of way. In fact, it is more like sculpture to me – adding to, taking away, and pushing into place. So I have sculpted a narrative of the life of my father, C. L. Whistler. When I was a child, I told him I would write his story, and he smiled. I would like to say the story is 100% true and correct. It is not. It is put together, pulled together, kneaded and stitched – depending on the metaphor you choose -- from the various anecdotes, jokes and memories he relayed to me and to others, as well as what I personally overheard or witnessed. The events I witnessed are true. I presume the ones he told to me are true as well, since he was an honest man, not given to shading the truth. And since he didn't account for every moment of his time, I was forced to fill in gaps by interpolation and a best, most probably guess as to what transpired. Those interpolations may or may not be true.

He was a not-so-simple cowboy from West Texas who really knew the likes of Joel McCrae and Dolores del Rio; who really made a raucous speech to a congregation of brush salesmen; who really built an automobile from junk parts at the age of 16; who really chauffeured a ne'er-do-well flim-flam artist to California; who really flew various aircraft and busted a bronco in the middle of traffic and all of the other things I have laid out in this book which I hope is a tribute to his memory and a celebration of his life.

He felt boasting was an earned right, and he seemed unaware – unconcerned, perhaps – of the resentment it stirred in others. "It ain't bragging if you can do it," he would say. Yet most who knew him described him as able, courageous and above all, good. His nephew Jim Edwards described him as "kind of exceptional." In celebrating Clyde Whistler's life through this narrative biography, I am indebted to the many sources on whom I relied for supplemental material, chief among them the Whistler family: Clyde Louis Jr., Dorothy and Beverly; and on his nieces and nephews: Jim Edwards, Bertha Edwards and Anna Bell.

# Chapter 1: It Was a Time

Wet, and shivering from the cold, lying behind a cluster of creosote bushes, bleary-eyed from lack of sleep, armed with only a 30-30 and a handful of cartridges, the young man watched the distant rider approaching along the mesa from the south, and wondered if he had heard the rifle shot. It had certainly been loud enough. The cow was a range cow. He had killed it with a single shot through the heart, and in doing so, the young man had committed the crime of rustling, which was a crime punishable by hanging if you were on the American side of the river, or by shooting if you were on the Mexican side.

The young man's name was Clyde Whistler. He was six foot tall and gaunt with straight dark brown hair that shone a reddish tint in the sun. He didn't appear particularly strong, but he was. He had scant body fat. He was fleet of foot, especially in mountainous, rocky or brushy environments. It was said he could run down a deer through sheer persistence and speed and doggedness. And now he was alone, cold and trapped just across the river on the Mexican side. The previous day's events had left him hungry, with neither clothes nor shoes. The river had taken them.

He watched the Mexican rider picking his way towards him through sagebrush and *ocotillo*, and as he surveyed his own situation, that the 100-foot limestone cliff was at his back and that he had nowhere else to go, there was nothing left to do but draw a bead on the approaching rider. He whispered a silent curse to a vague something – fate, perhaps – that had drawn him into this predicament. He wondered at what point he would pull the trigger. Then it occurred to him that maybe he wouldn't have to, that maybe the rider was nothing more than that – just a rider, someone who hadn't heard the rifle that fired into the heart of a range cow on this cold winter day. But as the rider drew closer, Clyde's heart sank. He was a Mexican border officer, a *federal*, and he rode with one hand on the stock of his rifle that poked out of the back of his saddle.

Dreading what was sure to follow as the final link in the chain of events of the past two days, he gave little notice that the rider wore a clean brown shirt on this most horrible of days, that he had a mustache which seemed a characteristic of Mexican men, and that his face was weathered and brown. Clyde pulled back the hammer on the 30-30 in the quiet way he was accustomed to in order to avoid alerting his quarry. He drew a bead, took a breath and steadied his grip. He waited. *"I'll give him to that twenty-yard mark,"* he said to himself. *"No, I'll give him to that 15-yard mark – that funny-shaped rock."* In his mind he drew an imaginary line from the rock to a cactus. *"He can't cross that line,"* he thought to himself. "*If he does, I shoot."*

Undeterred by Clyde's thoughts, the man continued riding, looking left and right as he came, drawing closer. Clyde watched him and noticed how unnaturally large he seemed and how loud the horse's hooves were as they struck small stones and crunched in the gravel.

As Clyde waited and as fifty yards became forty, then thirty, he wondered if he would have it in him to commit to the simple small act of pulling a lever. And he began thinking that this particular time was very nearly the worst in his life. The worst. There had been nothing like this before. The previous night had been one for the books: miserable, bitter cold, the wind whipping down the canyon, lightning all around followed by crackling waves of thunder. The river had risen so quickly it had forced him to try to either ford it get to the other side, which was Mexico, or to be broken against the canyon walls on the American side. He had crossed the river by carrying his clothes and a few provisions in a slicker, or raincoat, holding his rifle high above his head. But the river had suddenly taken the slicker and then dunked him and washed over him and almost drowned him. He had grabbed a log, then a rock, and had nearly slipped away again when his feet found the river bottom and he was able to struggle to the opposite bank, dog-tired and gasping for air. When he stood up at last, he noticed he had been clutching the rifle so hard his knuckles were white.

He sat and panted and stared at the churning brown water. "*It was a time,"* he thought. *"It was a time."*

The Mexican *federal* was within twenty yards now. Clyde fingered the trigger – but not enough to fire -- just to be reassured of its presence. He tensed his muscles. "*I hate to do this,"* he thought. His stomach shrank in anticipation.

The Mexican's horse almost stepped on the imaginary line; then, strangely, he stopped. He looked westward, wheeled his horse and rode away. Clyde exhaled. He watched him ride until he partially disappeared in the sagebrush and then dropped out of sight.

He would think of the incident many times later without fully understanding what had happened. He raised himself on one arm and maneuvered out of his hideout. Then he began to thread his way back down the cliff and eventually to the riverbank. Somewhere between here and there he hoped to find his lost clothes and supplies.

“*It was a time… It was a time,*” he said, and he kept repeating the phrase until it lost all meaning for him.

# Chapter 2: Return from the River

All in all, the fishing trip had been a wash. Clyde cussed his luck and the string of predicaments he had been thrown into, each one leading to another. But he didn't cuss the River. The River had taken his clothes and fishing tackle, and even the first few catfish he had caught; it had tumped him almost upside down in its muddy waters. But he didn't cuss the River. He feared it. It wasn't a scaredy-cat fear, but more like a respectful fear, the kind you'd have if you rode a bronco. You fear the beast, but not so much so you turn tail and run every time you see one. You ride it, knowing full well it could snap you like a twig. You ride it and you respect it, and you have something like love for it, but if you ever forget your fear for a minute, and if you forget the horse's tremendous power, you're a goner.

He had reached the American side and found that the River hadn't taken everything. There were trousers and a shirt within the brush where the now washed-out camp had been. They were soggy wet and muddy, but still wearable if he gave them a good rinsing. He did. He spread them out on a mesquite tree. With the help of the cool bottom breezes, they would dry soon enough.

He waited. And every now and then he threw a stick into the placid green water and watched the current carry it away. In the middle of the river a catfish jumped, probably a two-pounder. "Damn the luck," he thought.

When his clothes were dry enough, he pulled them on and made his way up the steep incline that led to where he had hidden his Model-T, or what he called his "hoopy." He pulled the cane stalks and creosote bushes away from it. Everything was as it should be. No one had bothered it. He kicked the chocks out from the wheels, took the crank out of the back, pushed it into the engine, and primed the cylinders with a couple of half-turns. Then he went back to the driver's seat to turn on the ignition key and throttle it before returning to give the crank a hard turn to the right (something you did left-handed in case the engine backfired and might break your arm). It started right up, just as he had expected it to do. He had built it with his own hands and knew what it could do. In spite of a sputter now and then, the car ran well. It had a *chugga-chugga* sound that was like music to his ears. He could get it up to 24 miles an hour on a level road, and by fiddling with the throttle on the drive shaft, and by going down a hill and around a curve, he could attain a scalding 26 ½ miles an hour. His hoopy was one of the major accomplishments in his young life and he was as proud of it as he could be.

It had come together from a pile of cast off parts in a trash pile. He was seventeen at the time. He had found a tire here, a flywheel, a distributor, a couple of pistons, wires, an axle there – and he had started playing with all the parts. He looked under the hoods of other autos to see how it all went together. Little by little, his own car started taking shape. It excited him to think that all this junk might run someday.

Meanwhile, the neighbors had become curious and had asked him what he was up to. When he said he was building a Model-T, they laughed. "When you gonna crank this thing up?" they would ask.

"When I get it ready," he would answer as he tightened a nut or followed a wire from the battery to the distributor.

Then one very hot day in July, with all the neighbors looking on, he told them it was time to try out his creation. Many chuckled; some pulled up chairs to get a ringside seat of Clyde falling on his face. He leaned his weight into the front of the car primed the engine. He turned on the ignition. He ran back to the front and cranked it. Nothing happened. Some of the neighbors laughed. He gave the crank another hard turn to the right and it sputtered, then caught.

The laughter died away. The small crowd stared in disbelief as he climbed onto the wooden front seat, put it in gear, pulled on the throttle, and sputtered off. He waved good-bye as he disappeared behind a house around the corner.

Hadn't it been like that time three years before he was born, back in 1908, when Wilbur (or was it Orville) had showed the doubting French that his contraption could fly? Pretty much like it. Not only did he show them it could fly, but he got it up in the air and flew around all day, circling, going away from them and returning and waving. And they praised him up and down afterwards.

His own little hometown episode had been pretty much like that.

Clyde thought about that time – his triumph – and he laughed to himself. And here he was again, sitting on the wooden bench that served as a driver's seat. After putting the auto into gear, he maneuvered the clutch and the throttle, and rolled off down the trail away from the river. It would be a rough and bumpy ride, but he would reach the main road soon enough. He had decided in advance he would go into town to see his mother. He felt he should. He would probably get there a little after dusk.

# Chapter 3: The Old Folks at Home

"It was hard to do, but I did it," Clyde told his mother, recounting the events of the past three days. He sat across from her, warming his hands around a cup of coffee. He was scratched and bruised. His mother didn't say much, but arose after a while to replenish the water in the tin cup she had set next to the fire to help humidify the house. A pendulum clock on the mantel -- a sort of spinning metal cylinder under a glass dome ticked incessantly. The top of the dome threw out soft reflections from the hurricane lantern. The clock was old. It had been with the family for as long as Clyde could remember, following them from town to town, always finding a home on the mantel. And it was never far from the three portraits on the wall above it.

The portrait on the left was an austere, elderly woman, Clyde's grandmother on his mother's side. Surely she was from a time far different from his own. She had a face that was at the same time stern and soft. And there was an underlying grittiness about her that as much as said, "Don't cross my path." Her face was a bit out of focus and her photograph was browning around the edges with age.

She contrasted sharply with the portrait on the far right, which was Clyde's father, John Whistler. He was a slight man, dapper and handsome. It wasn't his grittiness that showed through, but the look of a jokester. He had a wry sense of humor and there was little that he took seriously. One of his favorite pastimes was whistling. "If your name is Whistler, you should be good at it," he said, and taught the kids the same. He liked to make up absurd stories and act them out for days or months – years, if necessary -- as if they were true. He told all three of the Whistler children that he had once been a girl, but was quick to add that he hadn't particular cared for it.

He had worked as a young man on a spaghetti farm, he often told them, growing the damned stuff from daylight till dark. "Actually, it was a pretty good living," he would say. "Then they wanted to increase their profits, so they branched out and started making macaroni. The only thing macaroni was, was just spaghetti that had grown nice and fat, and you picked it and put a little hole in the middle. That was my job. I had to hold it still and then drill it right down the center. Well, that got kinda tiresome, and one day I got too smart for my britches. It was my idea to plant the spaghetti and then put a little piece of baling wire in the soil and let it just grow up around it. When it got big enough, all you had to do was pull out the wire and there you had some nice macaroni. Pretty smart! I worked myself out of a job, though. Once I gave them the idea for it, they didn't need me anymore, so naturally, they let me go..."

His portrait seemed to hold back the merest beginning of a smile, ready to spread into a grin as soon as the picture taking business was over.

In the center of it all was Clyde's mother. She was the one everyone called Biggun, or Big Mama, both names which she hated.

"What should the young'uns call you when they come along?" John Whistler had asked her one day. And she had replied in the spirit of the sternness of her mother that they could call her anything but 'Biggun.' But to say as much was to dangle a piece of bait in front of John that he couldn't resist. He took every occasion to turn the children's minds to calling his wife the name she liked the least. "Go ask Biggun," he would say. Or, "Where's Biggun? Go and find her." And the name stuck, of course.

In truth, her name was Bertha. She was a Hutchison and quite proud of it. She came from educated stock. She believed in the mystical. She believed thoughts have wings and that you can send them to people who are receptively inclined. Her portrait was a study in feminine beauty. She had coal dark hair and eyes. She posed in a freshly starched high-collar dress, her hair perfectly balanced high on her head. "Women wore their hair like that in those days," she liked to say. "Sometimes they used chains to hold it in place." And then she would always add, "*I* didn't."

Clyde had grown up feeling very lucky to have such a pretty mother. She seemed to him like an Esmeralda from the *Arabian Nights*. She was older than that now. He looked again into his still warm coffee. The fire popped and an ember arced onto the hearth and then died.

Her question had hung in the air. The seconds had ticked like so much dripping water. Had he been caught out in all that bad weather down on the river? He hadn't answered her directly.

"You went across the river, didn't you?" she said at last. He allowed as that was pretty much what happened.

"You don't have any business a-tall going across the river, Clyde."

"You're right, Mama," he said. He briefly looked up at the mantel and saw that the play of light on his grandmother's face wasn't entirely from the fire.

# Chapter 4: Born on Saturday

Clyde Whistler was born in Del Rio, Texas on August 19, 1911. The world he came into was already an atmosphere charged with invention, technological advancement and innovation. The telephone, the cinematograph and the automobile were new on the scene. Just three years earlier, Teddy Roosevelt was flexing America's muscle on the open seas, sending his Great White Fleet around the world; the Wright Brothers had demonstrated the feasibility of aircraft in the U.S. and in France; the Great Race – a world-wide automobile race featuring America's own creation, the *Thomas Flyer* – had kicked off in Times Square; Perry was headed for the North Pole; American engineers were cutting the continent in two at Panama; and Henry Ford introduced an affordable automobile called the Model T. In men's fashion, the straw hat was making a bold appearance, replacing the bowler. A man's dress suit could set the buyer back $25 at the finest stores. In May 1908 in Chicago, showgirl Bertha Carlisle, acting on a $500 wager with her manager, appeared in public wearing a form-clinging *Directoire* Gown from Paris and caused a near riot. Banks and businesses were using pneumatic tubes to ship timely documents; the vacuum cleaner appeared seemingly overnight; and about the time Clyde was born, a crackpot named Victor Appleton (some would say a prophet) was grinding out science-fiction potboilers that featured such mind-boggling inventions as an electric rifle (which fired electric bolts) and a picture telephone.

Yet Clyde was also born into a world with one foot firmly planted in the beliefs and superstitions of the Nineteenth Century and its "able nurses," home remedies and water witches. There were no doctors to speak of, or they were seldom seen. "Able nurses" delivered babies and knew herbal cures. They baked bandages, used sulfur and molasses, paregoric, boiled meat of a roadrunner for body sores, and made curative tea from a creosote bush. Turpentine and coal oil, or kerosene, would "draw the poison from a snake bite."[1]

He was born on Saturday, a Leo. He had a head of fiery red hair, an eager grin and grasping hands that seem to want to pull everything towards him. Leos, according to the Zodiac, possessed the attributes of confidence, ambition and a zest for life and that may or may not have been true in his case, but the fact was, he didn't believe in such silly stuff of superstition. He did believe, however, that a horsehair left overnight in a pond would become a snake. And he must have believed, if only for a short time, his father's story of how Clyde (or Clide, or Clid,

---

[1] Terrell County, Texas, Its Past – Its People, *Chapter Five*

as he spelled it, depending on his mood at the time) came to be the caboose, or last, of only three children in the Whistler family.

To hear his father tell it, when he and Biggun first married, they sat down together and worked out an agreement about how they would share the load of producing a family. She would have the first child, he would have the second, she the third, and so forth. Biggun stayed true to her part of the bargain and bore Johnnie. Next it was John's turn, and he had Zena. Then Biggun came right back at him with Clyde. When it was John's turn again, he thought about it and said, "I don't want no more." So they stopped with three children.

Clyde's earliest memory was of himself, sitting in a high chair and feeling extremely happy. Perhaps he was happy because of the new bright red shoes he wore. He stared at them and wiggled his feet. His parents had another early memory of him, and that was while they were on the way to Lordsburg, New Mexico and had a flat. John got out of the car to fix the tire, swearing under his breath, for this had been about the thirteenth time a tire had gone flat on the trip, and he heard a noise coming from the other side of the car. The noise was a clinking and a tapping sound, as if someone was trying to fit something to one of the lugs on the wheel. John walked around the back of the Model T and took a look to see what the noise was. It was Clyde, holding a tire iron with both hands, trying without success to remove the lug nuts from a perfectly good tire. He was barely five years old.

He may have been born in Del Rio, but considering how much John and Bertha moved around, he could just as easily have been born in Langtry, Sanderson, Marathon or any other little Southwest Texas town. Biggun could tailor and John could barber and that's what they did. But shortly after Clyde was born, Biggun developed a mastoid condition and felt she was unable to take care of one more child. From the time he was one year old until eleven, he spent more time with family friends and neighbors than with his own parents, eventually landing in the lap of his Aunt Esther and Uncle Terry Shely. Esther was quite fond of Clyde and wrote Biggun and John a letter offering to let the boy stay with them on their ranch in the Chisos Mountains, near the Big Bend.

"Why did you not send the children up here to me?" she wrote in a letter. "I could have kept them all..."

After Clyde had settled in at the ranch, Esther sent Biggun a postcard with the picture of an unknown child on the front. "Here is you a boy," the card read. "We will keep Clyde & you take this one..."

Clyde loved the ranch. It helped to form him. It was dry gravel creek beds and draws and headers; it was rock, cactus, ocotillo and creosote in patterns that repeated infinitely to the horizon; and it was a habitat for deer, javelina, polecat, rabbit, rattlesnake and coyote. His purpose in life, as he knew it at that time, was to go fearlessly into that terrain in search of his prey, no matter how far it ranged, and bring it back.

Biggun's health began to improve after her operation and she had just come up to the ranch for a visit and to bring Clyde clothes and provisions. He had asked her for more "cotridges" in a letter and she had obliged. His eyes widened on the prospect of the vast amount of prey he could now hunt with so much new ammunition.

"I'm afraid you're going to get lost out in these mountains, hunting and going and staying all day the way you do," Biggun said to him.

"I'll be all right, Mama," he said.

"What would you do if you got lost?"

"I won't get lost, Mama."

She stared at him long and hard. "Clyde, listen," she said. She was looking directly into his eyes as she held him by both small shoulders. "If you ever get lost, just find you a place to sit and sit down." There was a look of puzzlement on his face.

"Sit down and look all around you," she went on, "and think about your Mama. Look all around you and think about me and describe to me what you see. That way I'll know where you are."

"But I won't get lost," he insisted, still thinking of her strange antidote for it.

"Promise me, Clyde, that you'll do that." He promised.

The next afternoon he was hunting rabbit on the western slope when he flushed a deer. It was a big mule deer – the kind with the darkened snout and lower jaw and looks like a five o'clock shadow – and it was bigger than Clyde. It had a beautiful set of horns. All Clyde had was a .22, but maybe with luck, he could get close enough to it to bring it down, he thought. The buck bounded two or three times and then went into a header. Clyde followed, running as fast as he could, looking for a way to cut if off. He followed it, lost sight of it, and saw it reappear again, only to trot over the saddleback between the two mountains and vanish.

Clyde stopped to take a breather. He put the butt of his rifle on the ground and let the barrel support some of his weight. It was then that he noticed the sky and the faint glow in the west, the clouds changing color and going darker. Looking back behind him, where he had just come from, he noticed the fading sunlight hitting the tops of the ridges and none of it looked familiar to him. Had he run that far in search of the deer? Which way was the ranch house? He began walking back up through the header, trying to reach a vantage point so he could get his bearings. But following the header only led him into a box canyon, and he withdrew and retraced his steps once again.

By now the sun was setting and he could now see the evening star glowing high above the horizon. He had got out of the box canyon, but it had become too dark to make anything out of his surroundings and he still didn't know where he was, or how to find the way back home.

Remembering Biggun's words, Clyde sat down on a large rock. He would try to summon her. He scanned the horizon in a clockwise manner, tracing the outlines of the mountains with his eyes. He tried thinking of Biggun at the same time. "There's a big rock here," he thought to himself. "There's a dry creek bed and some craggy rocks over there. Further to the right of those rocks is the saddleback in the mountain, where the deer got away..."

He could see her face in his mind. He could almost hear her chuckling when she got Aunt Esther's card with a picture of that little boy on the front of it and Biggun reading the words aloud, "Here's you a boy. We'll take Clyde." He remembered the time when she took them all to the cinema and *The Great Train Robbery* was showing under the movie tent. A lot of folks were standing in line trying to get in and that created confusion around the entrance gate. So while Biggun was standing in line getting her change out of her purse, Clyde darted through the crowd, assumed a crouching position, looked all around, and was half way under the tent when he heard Biggun say, "And here's a dime for Clyde over there trying to sneak into the show."

"Aw, Mama!" he said, and walked over to the entrance gate to go in like honest folk. Once inside, he whispered, "I could have got in for *free*, Mama. And you had to go and tell on me."

"It isn't right, Clyde," she said, and led him, Johnnie and Zena down to some vacant chairs where they could sit and watch the movie.

He remembered her singing phrases of *Bangum* to him just before he fell asleep. "Bangum had a wooden knife," she would sing. And it would sound like a happy-go-lucky song for the first few lines and then it would change into something sad and foreboding towards the end of the verse.

*"Bangum had a wooden knife*
*Dillo-day. Dillo-day.*
*Bangum had a wooden knife*
*Dillo-day down.*

*Bangum had a wooden knife*
*He swore he'd take that wild boar's life.*
*Come away, cuddle down.*
*Killo-quay-quan..."*[2]

He remembered the painting of the wolf that always hung over her bed. It was a small picture. You practically had to climb onto the bed to see it. Once you did, you saw a winter scene of a lone wolf atop a hill at night, looking down on a farmhouse, everything covered in snow. All the lights in the houses were out. As the wolf looked down on the little group of houses, steam rose from its mouth. It always scared him a little. Why do you have this picture, Mama?" he asked her.

"I like it," she said. "It makes me feel cold.

Clyde's reverie broke. He was feeling a little chilly himself. Of course he hadn't thought to bring a jacket. He didn't think he'd be in the mountains after dark. He didn't know how long it had been since he first sat down on a rock in the little space, but for a second, he thought he noticed some of the rocks illuminated. Then light washed across them, and he could make out the *chugga-chugga* of a Model T in the distance. Someone had driven the automobile as far as they could off the road, had then killed the engine and had gotten out, walking directly towards the little place where he waited.

"Mama," he said, unbelieving. "Is that you?"

"Clyde," she hollered back. "Come out here."

He was really glad to see her. He grabbed his rifle and cartridges and bounded out of the little space. "How did you find me?" he asked.

"I just got a picture of where you were and got in the automobile and drove out here," she said. "You're sure a long way from the ranch house."

He never told her he had followed her instructions for summoning her, and he would never use such potent magic again, but would keep it mind if it were ever necessary. Years later, at a gas stop in Marathon, while answering the questions of an overly curious outlander from the East, he would point in the direction of the ranch that had once been his home and the distant Chisos Mountains and declaim to the shocked tourist, "I have hunted every imaginable wild animal over there: bear, wolves, javelina, mountain lions and mule deer. I have stepped on every rock in those Chisos Mountains; and the rocks I didn't step on, I [used as toilet paper].[3]

---

[2] See Appendix for the complete song of *Bangum*

[3] Paraphrased, *author*

# Chapter 5: The School Years

*My grade average in high school was almost as high as your body temperature.*

— *Clyde Whistler*

Biggun's operation a success, she and John took Clyde into their charge again about 1920. He still visited his uncle's ranch when he could, but trips were less and less frequent. Back with his parents, he attended school – three schools in seven years. Which school he was enrolled in depended on where his parents moved to next.

First it was Marathon, and that was a tough little place named after the Greek contests of centuries past, supposedly because of its resemblance to the Plains of Marathon. It faced mountain ranges on four sides and the adobe houses looked like a handful of dice tossed onto the plain. There were no paved streets, few fences, and it was hard to tell where one property ended and another began. Cough weed, or creosote, dotted the landscape and filled in the unused areas along and behind the houses. Wild burros ran free.

It was there that Clyde learned to take care of himself. He was several grades below his brother Johnnie. Johnnie had developed into a strapping youth so intimidating in musculature and size that no one bothered him much; he never worried about having to fight for his rank. Clyde, however, was slight like his father and invited the occasional mean challenge.

"I won't do your fighting for you," his brother told Clyde with an unemotional but certain tone of voice, "but I'll stand there and make sure it's a fair fight. I won't let anyone else in the fray. I think you could whip anybody your size in a fair fight, once I give you a few pointers. You win a couple, and there won't be anybody bother you anymore."

Johnnie taught Clyde the hook and the uppercut and how to hold his guard, and then let him go. "Don't telegraph your punches," he told him. "And don't throw any roundhouses."

And that was all fine, Clyde thought, but darned if he didn't have to fight just about every kid in town. Johnnie stuck to his word; he didn't fight Clyde's battles, and when Johnnie was standing there overseeing, the other kids all knew to keep it fair. But Clyde complained he had to fight half a dozen of them before they got the message that they weren't going to whip him.

He also fared well in academic subjects in Marathon, earning high marks in arithmetic, language, reading, spelling and writing; and mediocre marks in geography. The surprise to those who knew him was that he didn't fail English, for the little regard he held it. Math was pure and logical. English, on the other hand, was more rules than exceptions, and it sounded quaint and funny when it was supposedly spoken well. English – rather, *good* English – to Clyde, was a lot like "manners," which are pretty much useless, something you put on to impress folks in polite company and then take off the rest of the time.

And then, just as Clyde was becoming accepted in Marathon and getting used to school life, the family moved down the road to Sanderson, and then to Del Rio where he spent his high school years and bemoaned the fact that but for a quarter of a credit he was not allowed to graduate. You'd think they could have looked the other way for a quarter of a credit. But the administration wouldn't even consider it and no diploma ever came.

He had left his mark on the school, however, in old Mr. Adams' algebra class. He was the meanest teacher ever to walk through the front doors of the high school. He had an ancient, wrinkled prune face and thinning hair and he dressed like a military officer. He had pressed trousers and shirt. If he ever smiled, nobody heard tell of it. And it was Clyde's fortune to draw his class one semester. "The Old Man can be rough," the other classmates would say. And in the first week of class he had them all scared and shaky. He would send a student to the board to prove an equation and then interrupt him every time he opened his mouth. "How do you know that's true?" the Old Man would say, or "How can you make that statement?" The students were finally reduced to saying it was true because it *had* to be true, and that's kind of like that old boy that gets caught in a bull pen one day and there's no place to hide or any trees or anything, and suddenly he sees a bull coming at him, and he runs. But he's not as fast as the bull and the bull is gaining on him, getting closer and closer. And he can feel the bull's breath on the back of his legs. And the fellow he's telling the story to stops him and says, "What did you do then?"

And the old boy says, "Well, just as he was about to hook me…just as his horns were about this far from my fanny, I saw a tree and I climbed up it and saved myself."

And the other fellow thinks about the answer for a little bit and says, "Now wait just a minute! At the beginning of the story you said there *weren't* any trees. Now you say you got away from the bull by climbing up a tree. How's that?"

And the fellow telling the story looks at him and thinks the question over and says, "There *had* to be a tree."

Well, when those students got backed into a corner by Old Man Adams, and when they said the equation *had* to be true, they were as good as lost. They didn't have any proof.

Clyde swore a similar fate wouldn't happen to him. He went home and pored over every page in the algebra textbook until late in the evening. He went over and over the equations. Finally it hit him like a two-by-four between the eyes.

The next day, Old Man Adams said, "Mr. Whistler, come up here to the blackboard and write your answer to the third equation in the assignment and then prove it. Clyde was ready; he had just about memorized not only the chapter the assignment was from, but he had memorized the three preceding chapters as well. He picked up a piece of chalk and started writing the steps to the problem, which was to find the multiplication of integers 5 x 3. He scrawled neatly and purposefully:

5 x 3 = five threes
= 3+ 3 + 3 + 3 + 3
= 15

Old Man Adams interrupted him. "How do you know that?"

"By the commutative property," said Clyde.

"That doesn't tell me a thing," said Old Man Adams. "What's the commutative property?"

"The commutative property states that numbers can be added or multiplied in any order." The Old Man looked surprised. Then Clyde returned to his scrawling. Later, as Clyde was presenting another part of his proof, Old Man Adams interrupted him again.

"How do you know that?" he asked.

"The associative and distributive properties state that -- "

"Very good, Mr. Whistler," he said. "I can see that learning has taken place somewhere in this classroom."

The Old Man took a liking to Clyde after that, and Clyde did so well in algebra that he ended up with the highest average ever in algebra class in Del Rio High School. That was 97.5. Of course, he would have been happier if he had been given a diploma, but still he liked to brag that his grade record in Del Rio still held after twenty years – and that the highest record went to a poor cowboy they wouldn't even let graduate.

# Chapter 6: Jack Bailey

In the summer of 1931, not long after the Big Crash, Jack Bailey, known to some as Joe Clark for his own purposes, and to others as Wallace Wilkins, sat cleaning his fingernails in a café on the outskirts of Del Rio, Texas. He had little idea what his future was, but he was certain it wasn't in any of the places he had just come from, and where he was no longer welcome. He had been on the road for twenty days now, from Lake Charles over in the Bayou Country, across the state line to Beaumont, Texas and points west, finally ending up in this godforsaken little burgh near the Mexican border. His engine had overheated. He was aware it was nothing serious – nothing an hour or two of cooling down couldn't fix.

He sat at a well-varnished wooden table. When the waitress, who was a comely young lady of Hispanic descent, approached him, he smiled his top of the line smile at her and asked for lemonade – the sweeter the better. He quaffed it quickly, and then asked for another. He thought she took a shining to him. Most women did. He was tanned and good-looking, by most accounts. His hair was swept back from his forehead along a razor-sharp crease and was held neatly in place with generous applications of one of his very own all-purpose lotions he sold from the back of his car.

*"Cómo está?"* he said with a smile.

"You speak Spanish?" she said. "There is really no need..."

"Oh. I was thinking back to my Spanish classes in school, wondering how I could thank you for those deliciously cool lemonades for which I am much obliged. "I'm in your debt, young lady."

He tasted the lemonade and smiled his approval. "I am indeed in your debt...but wasn't it so the very first time I looked into those eyes of yours?" She had turned and started back to the counter, but paused. "How can I ever repay you for the beauty you have bestowed on one such as myself, a simple and humble knight of the road?" He nodded his head ever so slightly.

*"Caramba!"* she said.

As if searching for a way to repay her, his went to his shirt pocket. From it he retrieved first a small pouch of cut tobacco and then a small packet of cigarette paper. He removed a thin square tissue from the packet and sprinkled a bit of tobacco into the crease. She watched as he licked one edge of the tissue and then rolled it between his two fingers.

He glanced up at her. "What's your name, darlin'?" he asked.

"Rosalinda."

"Rosa-leenda," he repeated. "Desert flower – beautiful name – rolls off the tongue. Gorgeous...mellifluous."

"It really just means 'pretty rose,'" she said.

"Oh, it does?" he said. "Well, say, Rosalinda, do you have a match about you?"

"No."

"Lean a little closer," he said. "I think I see one behind your earring. He reached towards her, touched her ear, and brought his hand back with a match between his fingers.

Her eyes widened. She emitted an audible gasp. Then he smiled at her and lit his cigarette. "Much obliged, darlin'," he said.

She took a step back, wanting to say something, but not knowing what. "How did you do that?" she asked at last. "I don't carry any matches."

"I don't know," he said. "Could be magic, maybe." She touched her ear. "By the way, my name's Jack Bailey." Smoke drifted up from the cigarette and then curled into itself and disappeared. He exhaled. "I'm headed west – far, far west – maybe even so far as Hollywood, California."

"Really?"

"Yeah. You know what the man says, 'Go west, young man.' I'm taking his advice."

"What do you do? Magic?"

"Oh, no. Various things…sales mainly...I'm in sales."

He passed part of the afternoon by exchanging a word or two with Rosalinda whenever she passed by his table. At length, he pulled an old watch from his vest pocket, stared at it, and pushing three dimes towards Rosalinda for his drinks, rose to leave the café. "I'll be moving along now," he said.

On his way out the door, he stopped. "Oh, by the way," he said. "What's the next little burgh up the road from here, if I'm heading due west?"

"There's lots of little stops along the railroad," she answered. "About five or six of them. And then you'll come to a town called Sanderson. It's a long ways from here."

"Much obliged, ma'am. And if I ever come back this way, I'll drop in for another glass of your lemonade." He tipped his hat and walked towards his automobile. After starting it, he pulled it onto the dusty road and headed west. Soon the road became smoother and flatter, and he opened the throttle up. The effect of the air on his face felt good. It cooled him.

As he drove, he began humming the first few bars of the popular jazz tune, *Bill Bailey*, and made up his mind that 'Bailey' would be the name he would use, at least for a while.

# Chapter 7: Young Man Heads West

In the summer of 1931, at the age of 20, Clyde worked as a cowboy. Work was scarce, yet he managed to get small jobs riding herd, shearing and dipping sheep. When the ranch work was available, sheep shearing paid about one-and-a-half cents a sheep, but it was seasonal work and never lasted for more than a week or two. Dipping sheep involved herding sheep single-file into large concrete troughs filled with an exactly proportioned mixture of water and arsenic-laced insecticide to kill parasites.[4] It was sweaty, smelly, dirty work and came in last place among the jobs to do on a ranch.

When work on the area ranches played out, Clyde would find odd jobs in the various train-stop towns along the Southern Pacific route from Del Rio to Marathon. When carpentry work was available, he hired out as a carpenter's apprentice; at other times, he found work as a general laborer mixing and pouring concrete. He strove to be a "dollar-a-day" man, yet he often settled for half that amount. None of the work paid enough to keep body and soul together, because paid wages had dropped so low during the first years of the depression.

Once, after breaking horses on a ranch near his uncle's place in the Chisos, Clyde was riding his horse into Tesnus when he spotted a Model T ahead of him. His horse, a range horse, had never been around the mechanical contraptions, and Clyde began to brace himself for the worst, fearing the horse would react poorly, and wondering just how he would handle the situation. The normal *chugga-chugga* sound of the Model T paused, and the black machine began to emit a sound like a cauldron boiling, quickly morphing into a low-pitched growl. The horse skittered. Then the car engine backfired, blowing off a piece of the muffler. And with that, all hell broke loose.

The horse pitched skyward. Clyde gripped the reins closer to the saddle horn, and held tight. Cars stopped. People gathered to watch. Some cheered and slapped their hats against their legs. Clyde stayed with the bronc as it did everything but turn belly up to the sun. He could hear someone in the crowd say, "Ride 'em, cowboy!"

He was scared and excited at the same time. He remembered above it all that it was his will against the horse's – and that he, Clyde, would win in the end. And he did. At length, the bronc stopped the fight and Clyde was able to ride it in a normal fashion. "I should've charged 'em a nickel apiece," he said later, referring to the passersby who had stopped to witness the exhibition. "I'll bet I could've made a day's wages for ten minutes' work."

---

[4] Terrell County, Texas, Its Past – Its People, *Chapter Two*

He was a young man still, and full of ambition, and he was certain the western horizon held the answer to his dreams. He had often heard the quote from that famous newspaper editor – Greeley, he thought his name was – that a young man should go West. And the more he heard about California, and the more movies he saw, the more the west coast took on the aspects of an El Dorado, or City of Gold. He had heard of Sutter's Mill and the great Gold Rush of 1849, and who knew but that a person might be able to find gold in those hills even in modern times, and even during the Depression, provided the person knew where and how to look for it. And if the state was built on gold, there was probably a lot of money around and plenty of opportunity for a young man. Hollywood beckoned to him from a great distance, and the call grew louder and stronger with each new passing day.

"You never know," he thought to himself. "I might find my fortune there."

Towards the end of June, when the thought of going west was all but devouring him, Clyde paid a visit to his mom in Sanderson. He pulled up in front the house, cut his motor and stepped out onto the pathway leading to the house. He passed under the breezeway, scraped his boots on a boot blade, and rapped at the screen door. It rattled on its hinges. "Mama!" he called out. He opened the door and stepped into the kitchen where she had just finished putting up some preserves and was preparing a pot of coffee.

She poured him a cup. "What do you know good?" she said, and they talked. Clyde relayed how things were around different parts of the Big Bend country, who got rain, who lost sheep, and who he had seen in Marathon. During the course of the conversation, he said a few words about the bucking bronco episode, all of which caused his Dad to smile. "I broke a mean 'un over in Tesnus," Clyde told him. "And never got paid a lick for it."

"That's what happens," said his dad. "Wouldn't have drawed much if you did get paid for it." Clyde nodded agreement.

On the wall in the living room, the three portraits stared at him over the hurricane lamp on the mantel, as always. Beyond them, over a single bed, hung the painting of the Lone Wolf, breathing steam into the cold winter air while he contemplated the ranch house below him, as always.

"Mama," Clyde said at length, "There's a guy who says, 'Go West, young man, and find your fortune.' And I'm a young man. And I b'lieve that's what I'm gonna do."

"Well," said Biggun. "You won't have to go far – at least, not more than a step or two."

"What --?" said Clyde.

“You’re living right here in the West now,” she said, “So you don’t have to take the man’s advice.” Clyde caught a glimpse of his father smiling behind his paper.

“I mean really far west, Mama. Over in California.”

“That far,” said Biggun and arranged her spoon on a napkin. “Well, how do you propose to get there?”

“I don’t know,” said Clyde. “I’ll find some way. But I wanted to tell you about it. I’ve been thinking it over for a while now and it sounds like a pretty good thing to me. Maybe I’ll work my way over there, or maybe I’ll catch a train and sit in a boxcar like I see all those people doing out at the train station, down on their luck.”

“Oh, don’t be like those folks!”

“I’ll find a way somehow,” said Clyde. “Something will come along.”

Two days later, almost as if by answered prayer, Clyde came across a car stuck in a bar ditch five miles outside of Sanderson. The driver, who was apparently an outlander, was sitting on a rock, holding his head in his hands. He scarcely saw Clyde pull up and get out of his Model T.

“Are you all right?” asked Clyde.

“I’m okay, but I can’t move my car,” said the man, moving the thick black strands of hair from his eyes.

Clyde walked all around the car and surveyed the damage. Then he whistled.

“Is it that bad?” asked the stranger.

“No, it ain’t bad a-tall,” said Clyde. “I was just admiring this touring car. It’s a mighty nice one.”

“You think so?” asked the man.

“Yep.” The left hood was ajar and Clyde peeked inside. He whistled again, almost inaudibly this time.

“I was coming around that bend in the road and the sun got in my eyes,” said the stranger. “The sun blinded me and the next thing I knew, I was in the ditch. I’m none the worse for wear, though.” Clyde was already walking away from the car, reaching into the back of his own car and pulling out chain and rope while the man talked.

“I’ll get you out,” he said. He looped the chain and rope together and ran one end under the front axle of the touring car. Then he tied it to the Model T and drew out the slack. Within minutes he was pulling the touring car out of the ditch to a point where all four wheels touched the ground.

“Now you can start it up and drive out,” he said. “Trouble with these cars is, if three wheels are on the ground and the fourth one is even so much as a half-inch in the air, it won’t budge a-tall. You’re all set now. You can go.”

"Wait a minute," said the stranger. "I'd have never got the car out of the ditch if you hadn't shown up. I want to thank you." He extended his hand. "My name's...Jack Bailey. What's your name?"

"Clyde Whistler," he said, tossing the chain back into the car and dusting off his hands. He threw a glance over one shoulder in the general direction of town. He pulled a bandana from his back pocket to mop his brow. "Pleased to make your acquaintance."

The two of them talked for half an hour or so, and during that time, Clyde learned that Jack Bailey was a businessman out of Washington State, that he was the owner of a big department store there, and that he was on his way back home, via California.

"It's California or bust!" he said with a big grin. "That's me."

"Is that right?" said Clyde. "Well, I'm going to have to be getting along," I'd like to go west myself, but I need to find a way to do it."

"You got a job, Clyde?" asked Jack, stopping him.

"Not right at present. I'm kind of between jobs."

"You're pretty good around cars, aren't you?" continued Jack.

"Well, yes. I know a thing or two about 'em."

"Like I said a while ago, Clyde, I'm much obliged to you for getting me out of this scrape, and I'd like to repay you, if I could. How'd you like to come with me to California as my chauffeur? I think we'd do fine together."

Clyde wasted no time in accepting the offer, even though it was from someone he hardly knew. Opportunity in the form of free passage to California had come knocking, and he was not going to turn it away. He went to settle up his possessions and gather his things for the trip, and then went by the Folks' house to give them the news. His sister Zena happened to be there as well. As Clyde bade them all good-bye, he bent over and whispered to Zena that she might want to watch the local paper in a day or so, and that if she did, she just might come across some news about him.

She did as he said. Two days after Clyde struck out for California with his new boss, an article appeared in the Sanderson Times near the back page:

**LEAVES FOR WEST COAST**

Clyde Whistler, son of Mr. and Mrs. John Whistler, left Sunday for points on the west coast, having accepted a position as chauffeur for Jack

Bailey, salesman, and owner of a large department store in Spokane, Wash. While nearing this city last Friday night Mr. Bailey went to sleep at the wheel of his car which left the road and was badly damaged. It was after this accident that he engaged Clyde to travel with him.

# Chapter 8: Points West

*A peddler...also known as a canvasser, cheapjack, monger, or solicitor (with negative connotations since the 16th century), is a traveling vendor of goods...*

*Peddlers usually traveled on foot, carrying their wares, or by means of a person- or animal-drawn cart or wagon (making the peddler a hawker).*

*Modern peddlers may use motorized vehicles to transport themselves and their commodities. Typically, they operate door-to-door or at organized events such as fairs.*

*While peddlers had a significant role in supplying isolated populations even with fairly basic and diverse goods such as pots and pans, horses, and news, their market share has in modern times been drastically reduced as increasing density of population and buying power encouraged sedentary, even specialized sales points, while modern transport, mail order, refrigeration and other technology allow even rural clients alternative channels of purchase.*

*In the United States, the era of the traveling peddler probably peaked in the decades just before the American Civil War. The large advances in industrial mass production and freight transportation as a result of the war laid the groundwork for the beginnings of modern retail and distribution networks. Further, the rise of popular mail order catalogues (e.g. Montgomery Ward began in 1872) offered another way for people in rural or other remote areas to obtain items not readily available in local stores.*[5]

Bailey had made a deal with Clyde, and the deal was that he would pay Clyde for his services in full once they reached California. Pay would be based on the going wage for a chauffeur, which was better than the usual wages for working as a cowboy. In the meantime, Bailey would provide room and board for Clyde, although "room," (as Clyde would discover) might entail pulling off the road to sleep on the ground, and "board" might be construed as stopping in some town along the way for a sandwich or eating meals that could be cooked over a campfire. At times, Clyde wondered if he had struck a bad deal, or if maybe he had been too eager to take any deal so long as it meant heading towards California. He would have plenty of time to mull it over.

They had departed Sanderson around noon. Once they were on the road, Jack Bailey had talked freely. He had been happy to have company on the long trip, and to forego the tedious task of driving, and to be able to put his feet out the window,

---

[5] Wikipedia

and feel the summer wind in his toes, and lean back and rest or even sleep while the car moved across Texas.

Clyde noticed that Bailey could be a charming fellow, and that his charm and wit were quite endearing. He also seemed a well-educated man, fond of dropping fifty-cent words as he talked. Sometimes he talked to Clyde, and other times to himself. No matter who Bailey was talking to, Clyde found him a little hard to follow, and that was most of the time. And there were other times when Clyde couldn't make head nor tails of what Bailey was saying. Of course, he couldn't let on like he didn't understand, so when he heard words like "volubility" and "volatility" and phrases like "business climate" which seemed to have nothing to do with weather, Clyde would just stare ahead at the road and nod understandingly. About half way across Texas, Clyde could say with certainty that he never knew a man who could talk so much (and say so little).

Sometimes Bailey would go on and on, and then grow quiet, and look out the window and just think for a while. There would be long moments of silence, and then he would begin to hum – very softly at first, and then more loudly. Soon he would be singing the tune he loved – the one that sounded close to his own name – singing it as if he didn't care who heard him:

I'll wash the dishes, honey
I'll pay the rent
I know I done you wro-ong...

And so the trip would go as the highway unfurled mile after mile of scenery with endless sagebrush, cactus, mesquite, cough weed and limestone rock rolling by as if on a backdrop loop in a movie. Barbed wire fences ran alongside both sides of the highway, and the Southern Pacific railroad tracks on the left. When Clyde and Bailey passed a train, it was not uncommon for them to see freebooters leaning out from the boxcars, peering as far as they could up the tracks to see what lay ahead.

As he drove through the Big Bend area, Clyde's eyes fell on the majestic blue mountains to the south. He remembered his youthful days there, hunting from dawn till dusk on the big range of the Chisos, walking over those mountains, "stepping on every rock there," as he liked to say, seeing up close the volcanic rock formations, and the antelopes grazing in the foothills, and he found himself wishing he had brought his 30-30 and a box of cartridges so that he could travel back to that time and walk the draws and relive his youth, if only for an hour or two. But he was a chauffeur now.

He pressed a little harder on the gas pedal, and was pleased with the responsiveness of the wonderfully equipped touring car and how it seemed to move effortlessly over the long stretches of highway.

Like the road, Clyde's mind would wander. The road followed the old Butterfield Stage route, turned now into a highway. It wound through the mountains of Alpine and Van Horn, and into the further reaches of the bosky country just outside of El Paso.

The two men might stop for gas and a sandwich and a cup of coffee, or Jack might decide a place was a nice "locale" to "proffer some of his wares." He had a lot of items to sell – from hair pomade to fancy shirts and dresses. Clyde noticed that his employer could be very persuasive in selling. People, most often ladies, would buy from him based on his wit and charm, and probably because of his good looks. And of course, it didn't hurt sales when he threw in an unsolicited magic trick or two. But Clyde also noticed that Bailey never wanted to hang around after he folded up shop.

He watched Bailey often enough to pick up his sales techniques (magic tricks notwithstanding) and he learned from the man how to properly fold a shirt so that it looked like it had been done in the factory. And he noticed that Bailey was able to establish a rapport with his customers and create a relationship in which they felt they were buying from a friend rather than a total stranger. All in all, even if Clyde hadn't seen a single dime yet for his services, he was receiving a valuable education, of sorts.

After about a week of traveling, the two men approached Lordsburg, New Mexico. Just seeing the sign was enough to cause Clyde's heart to shrink in his chest. He had a feeling of deja-vu and it wasn't the pleasant kind. It had been so long ago. He had been there with his parents when just a child. The trip had turned a normally happy-go-lucky John Whistler into an angry, swearing person Clyde hardly recognized. First one tire would go flat, and then hardly a mile would go by and another tire would go flat. It would have been comic if it had happened to someone else. It was just the sort of predicament Clyde had seen Charlie Chaplin get into in the days of silent film. But real life wasn't all that funny. At one point, Biggun held Clyde's ears to keep him from hearing his father's profanity and carrying on.

Clyde had long forgotten the reason behind the trip to New Mexico, traveling along the old Butterfield Stage route to a distant, Godforsaken town at the edge of the world, but he never forgot the trip itself. And he never forgot that they had fourteen flat tires in the short distance of ten miles, and how Fate, or the gods, seemed to be having sport with them. Even as a young boy, he thought that particular adventure must have been what Hell was like – the never-ending trip, and a seemingly infinite number of menial hot and sweaty tasks.

Actually, Lordsburg was one of two prime injustices in his life. It was simply a case of man against the elements, and the elements beating him down and reducing him to a profanely swearing and complaining animal. The other injustice was man versus man and all the more stinging since it involved a charming, youthful and enthusiastic scoutmaster and a breach of trust.

There had been a scoutmaster when Clyde was a boy, who had virtually promised him and his scout troop the moon if they would only get out and apply a little elbow grease and raise some money. They were to go on a grand and glorious field trip and camp out for days in some wilderness park and do all sorts of fun things Boy Scouts enjoyed doing. Clyde was a damned good scout. He loved the activities, and he believed in the scoutmaster. Clyde worked harder than anyone else to raise the funds for the trip. Like them, he cleared yards and cleaned houses and washed windows and cars.

But on the day the scoutmaster had promised to meet with the boys and discuss how the money they had raised would be spent, he simply disappeared. The 37 dollars (quite a sum in those days) was gone too. The deception and betrayal hurt Clyde to the quick.

As he and Bailey continued along the highway, Clyde's mind drifted back to other more pleasant memories of his youth, and he found himself already missing the family. He missed the antics of his father, the ready wit of his mother, and the various things Zena and Johnny got themselves into. The touring car drove on, and all the old memories began to work themselves into his mind.

Clyde thought of his mother and how she always seemed to be there to help him out of trouble. And he thought of the time he had pulled his Hoopy up in front of the house to work on the engine – he didn't remember what exactly he was doing, but it was something that required a screwdriver and him holding tight to one end of the engine block and trying to force the screwdriver under a gasket, and suddenly the screwdriver slipped and drove straight into his wrist.

He didn't feel any pain – just a sensation something like bumping the funny bone on his elbow. And then a tiny stream of blood shot straight up, ten feet in the air, pumping in spurts, and he gazed at it, like it had happened to someone else and not himself. "Mama!" he called. "Would you look at this?"

Biggun had just stepped out the front door when he called her. "Land sakes, Clyde!" she said. "You'll bleed to death." She put a tourniquet around his arm and "adjusted" his shoulder and upper back until the bleeding stopped.

When it did, at last, she caught her breath, and had time to think, and scolded him. "If you had died, you'd certainly have gone happy," she said. "I never saw someone so interested in their own blood as you. You know you don't have an endless supply, Clyde."

He could almost hear her in his mind as he drove, saying, 'Land sakes!' and the thought brought a smile from him.

He thought of his father the relentless teasing and how much his father enjoyed it, and didn't know when to stop. He thought about himself and Johnny, and how they had learned to deal with it their father's teasing, but Zena hadn't and the teasing drover her to the point of distraction. Clyde remembered that his sister, this otherwise most kind and most gentle person on earth once found a family photo, and took a pencil in her fist, and stabbed it into the face one of the subjects, which happened to be John Whistler. She probably felt vindicated, and he probably laughed, and maybe he even changed his ways after seeing the effect his teasing had had on her. And then again, maybe he didn't.

Clyde's thoughts turned to Johnny and his conversation with a stranger in a bar, and the diminutive stranger looking up at Johnny, and holding up his glass and saying, "You know what? If I was big and strong like you, I'd go out and find myself a big ol' bear and wrestle him down to the ground! That's what I'd do..." Calm and unruffled as always, Johnny just looked at the stranger and said, "There's lots of little bears around..."

Yet when backed into a corner, Johnny did indeed tangle with wild animals. He drew his .45 at the edge of a precipice and killed an eagle in mid-flight as it swooped to attack. And once, while hunting with dogs, he crawled into a cave to rest. He had no way of knowing it, but a mountain lion was in the cave, and as Johnny entered, the lion came bounding out. It jumped over him. As it did, he shot and killed it. He kept the lion's hide as a memento of the adventure.[6]

A startled covey of quail burst into the air at a turn in the road, and Clyde came out of his reverie. He noticed once again the growl of the road under the tires of the touring car and the smooth sound the engine produced. What a joy it was to drive such an automobile. The evening air felt cooler on his face and the western sky was dimming. All the while, Jack slept under his hat, leaning his head against the window and the rest of his body pressed into the corner of the seat and the door.

After crossing the border into Arizona, it occurred to Clyde that they hadn't had so much as a single flat tire this time around. He wondered what his dad would have thought of that.

---

[6] Terrell County, Texas: Its Past, Its People. Chapter 7

In Arizona, they drove through Tombstone, and then rested at the little town of Bisbee. It was a picturesque little town and Clyde remembered thinking it might be a nice place to stay for a while, if he weren't otherwise engaged as a chauffeur. He noticed the mines and all the attendant mining activity, and made a mental note that perhaps he could come looking for work in the pleasant little community if things didn't go well in California.

They had covered a thousand miles by mid-July. They had driven the open highway and camped in the desert when necessary. Sometimes Jack sold goods in the small towns they passed through. Often he flirted with the ladies and seemed to enjoy amazing them with his sleight-of-hand while he talked about his wares. Clyde wondered how much farther the West Coast could be. It seemed forever. Nevada would come next, and with it, Las Vegas. Then, at long last, they would cross the border into California and head for the famed city of Hollywood.

So once again, they set out, Clyde driving while Jack lay in the back seat, putting his bare feet out the window, and pulling his hat over his eyes to go to sleep. "Wake me in Vegas," he said. "I've got some people I need to see there."

# Chapter 9: The Meadows

After traveling for miles across Arizona and the northern edge of the Chihuahua Desert, Clyde and Bailey entered a basin with mountains on either side. The road was straight but uneven in elevation, and where it was uneven, water mirages would appear, hover just above the ground, and seemingly evaporate. It was unbearably hot that day, and the mirages looked so convincing and of such a cool sky blue that Clyde sorely wished they were real. Where he might see one, Bailey wouldn't; and where Bailey would ask, "Is that water up ahead?" Clyde would fail to see it. After a while they began to ignore them, assuming that anything up ahead that resembled a pool of water, wasn't.

Then, at a distance, Clyde saw it – the small, indistinct something stretching across the highway, rippling in the heat, so bright and full of light that even in the afternoon sun, it glimmered. It lay flickering like a flame above the pavement and consuming itself.

This, thought Clyde, must be Las Vegas. Yet he wasn't entirely sure it wasn't just another mirage. He kept his eye on it as he drove; the mirage didn't vanish. It even began to spread outward, growing in size. Clyde felt his shirt cling to his back, and in an attempt to get more comfortable and benefit from the movement of the open air, he shifted in his seat. He turned to Bailey but to alert him of the sight, but there was no need. Bailey had seen it as well. He stared ahead.

"Hmmh! That's it," he grunted. "That's Las Vegas." He shot a glance at Clyde. "Does this look like meadows to you?" he asked.

"Meadows?" said Clyde. "No, I wouldn't describe it that way. Why?"

"Because that's what Las Vegas means," said Jack. "This used to be meadows around here. Cows grazed." Jack squinted into the sun. He bowed his back and yawned. "Gambling's legal here now, you know," he went on. "'Course, it doesn't matter whether it's legal or not, it's always been around, under cover, like. Like the speakeasies where you can get liquor right in the middle of Prohibition. And they've got speakeasies, here too in Las Vegas. Seems like everything's legal here – probably because the city wanted to capitalize on all those government workers over there on the dam – Boulder Dam or Hoover Dam or something like that." Bailey removed his hat and wiped the perspiration from his forehead with a clean white handkerchief. "When you get into town a little, turn down Fremont Street and we'll stop at a little watering hole there."

"So you've been here before, then?" asked Clyde.

“Plenty of times,” said Jack. “But it sure has grown. I don’t remember it like this, or even this active.”

The highway led into Fremont Street, where there was a traffic light. It was the first Clyde had ever seen. Cars were everywhere – either on the street taking turns at intersections, or parked in lots. And there was advertising. Big signs advised smokers that Chesterfields wouldn’t make them nervous, or that Luckies were “fresher.” On the side of one red brick building was an immense comic character that smiled and held a wand and watched a disk the size of Clyde’s head, bubbling in a glass of water. “FEEL SWELL WITH ALKA-SELTZER!” the character said. “Boy, that’d be some headache!” said Clyde.

Through an alleyway he saw – or thought he saw – a giant cowboy statue standing beside a two-storey building. Then Clyde rounded the corner and saw the big 50-foot structure in all its glory. It looked like something out of the funny papers. It was tall enough to give you a crick in your neck, and it was the type of cowboy Clyde would have referred to in earlier days as “drugstore,” or dressed for show. The big cut-out cowboy leered. He wore a bandanna. A cigarette dangled from his mouth, and he sported a starched red-checkered shirt. His thumb was pointing over his shoulder in the direction of the nearby Pioneer Casino building. “THIS IS IT!” said the sign

“Ain’t that sumpin’?” said Clyde. Just then a traffic light came out of nowhere. It surprised him; he ran through it, turning the wrong way down a one-way street. Another motorist honked at him, and Clyde threw up his hands as if to say, “Don’t shoot!” and the other motorist laughed. A young painted woman sat beside the man. She laughed too.

The sidewalks were crowded with people strolling or ducking into casinos and bars. Street lamps twelve feet tall ran along the avenues. Bailey took one look and said, “Glitter Gulch.”

“Well, it is certainly glittery,” thought Clyde, considering that in the span of two minutes he had seen more traffic lights, neon lights and street lights than he could have imagined anywhere else but inside an issue of Life Magazine. Neon facades informed him there was “Gambling Inside,” that the establishment was a “House of Jackpots,” that he was at the Dixie, the Apache, the Northern, or the Las Vegas Club, and that inside he could obtain “Liquor,” and that parking was FREE.

“Ain’t this sumpin’?” said Clyde. He drove in low gear at a snail’s pace in order to take it all in. He could hear music. From inside a parlor on one street, the radio was playing “Hey, brother can you spare a dime?” while on other streets, groups of rough-looking men squatted and stood in line outside a building. “Is that a soup line?” Clyde asked.

"Nope," said Bailey. "Those poor suckers all hope they can get a job working at the dam up the road – Boulder Dam up Highway 91." After a bit, Bailey pointed to a brightly-lit building decked out in running lights and said, "Can you turn in here at the Apache and park in back?" A life-sized wooden Indian was stationed at the base of the steps. Cattle skulls lay next to wagon wheels. Doorways and windows were marked off with lariats, and spurs were hammered onto walls.

Clyde drove past a couple of fully-developed prickly pears through a wrought-iron gate and pulled the car into one of the lanes, painted just for parking. He pulled alongside another touring car, shinier than Bailey's. A well-dressed young man with coal-black hair leaned on the front fender, crossing his arms.

"Wait here," said Bailey. "I've got some business to attend to inside. Don't let anyone steal my car. I'll be back out in a bit." He smiled.

Clyde put on the emergency brake, opened the door and stepped out. It was the first chance he had had to straighten his legs since early that morning. He looked around, yawned and stretched. While Bailey walked around to the front of the building, the well-dressed young man watched from the corner of his eyes.

# Chapter 10: Strange Confession

The well-dressed young man leaned nonchalantly against his car and folded his arms. Perhaps he too was a chauffeur, Clyde thought, and paid him no mind after that. Whatever the case, they both were waiting for someone inside.

Clyde reached into his trouser pocket and retrieved a jack knife and a whetstone. He opened the knife and began to sharpen it in careful circular motions, first in one direction and then the other. He valued the knife, a Barlow. He depended on it in so many ways and he took an overweening pride in its upkeep. And he took almost as much pride in maintaining the whetstone, which cost about twenty-five cents many years ago, and which he had no intention of replacing for years to come. He kept it so evenly worn that it was almost like the original, only smaller in size.

He glanced at his watch, a Bulova. It was a bracelet watch – easy on and easy off – and it was a fine timepiece at that. It kept very accurate time. He had bought it in El Paso when he and Bailey were passing through. It had a bright red second hand as thin as a human hair that moved fluidly above the dial. The copper bracelet flashed orange in the sun.

"What time is it?" the young man asked.

Clyde didn't answer at first. After a moment, he glanced at his watch. "Quarter to four," he said.

"Been kinda warm today, hasn't it?" asked the young man.

"Um-hm," Clyde said. He half-ignored the young man, and ran his thumb across the blade of his knife. Then he folded it with a click and put it back in his pocket.

"Do you gamble?" the young man asked.

"Maybe," said Clyde, a little annoyed.

"Oh, I'm sorry," said the young man. "Really I am. I'm just sitting here asking you one question after another like you were one of those coin-operated fortune tellers." He smiled and scratched his head. "I don't have any kind of upbringing at all," he continued. "Let me introduce myself. My name's Charlie. Charlie...Smith. Charlie Bowman. My name's Charlie Bowman." He stuck out his hand. "What's your name?"

"Clyde Whistler."

"Charlie Bowman," he said again. "I am pleased to make your acquaintance. Is that your boss that went inside?"

"He's not really my boss," said Clyde.

"Oh. You fellas aren't from around here, are you?"

"I'm not," said Clyde.

"You gamble?"

"No. Not really. It doesn't interest me." Clyde could have said much more on the subject, if he had wanted to, but didn't. He still wasn't comfortable talking to a virtual stranger, especially not outside a casino that was lit up like the Fourth of July. He could have told the young man about Biggun and how she loathed gambling, and how she said it had been the ruin of many an otherwise good man, and how she desired very strongly for all her children to be failures at the sport. He could have told the man about the curse – or what had amounted to a curse – Biggun had put on him and Johnny to discourage them from pursuing games of chance as any means of increasing their wealth. With the curse, he could never win, so there was really no point in it. It was probably a wasteful pastime. At any rate, he related to the stranger that he simply had no interest in it.

"Well, that's a good thing," said the young man.

The two stood quiet for a while, not saying anything. Clyde looked around, taking in the city, and a couple of times his eyes fell on "Big Tex," leering and pointing to the Pioneer Casino. "There's lots of gambling around here," said the young man at last. "In fact, that's all there is here – well just about all."

"It doesn't appeal to me," repeated Clyde.

"That's good," said the young man. "It's not a habit you really want to get started. You could end up out in the desert with a bullet in your head."

"What?" said Clyde.

"Gambling can kill you," said the young man. He took out a packet of Chesterfields, tapped one into his hand, and lit it. "I've been on the other end of that predicament on several occasions – none of them happy."

"Do you mean as a gambler?" said Clyde.

"No, as a driver." He saw that Clyde looked puzzled. "I'm a driver for the mob," he said, smiling and blowing a smoke ring. "Did you guess?"

"No," said Clyde.

"How can I say this without sounding too crude?" He flicked ashes from the cigarette. "I have driven men to their death, just for not paying up on a gambling debt."

"What do you mean?" asked Clyde.

"I mean, my boss and some other guys would collar some poor fellow who was in arrears to them, invite him to go on a ride with them, me driving, and they'd tell me to go out to the desert and park the car and wait. And that's what I'd do, and I'd hear a pistol shot, and then after a while, they'd come back and tell me to drive them somewhere else. They didn't have to tell me to keep my mouth shut – I already knew that. Hell, I shouldn't even be telling you this stuff..."

"No, I guess not," said Clyde. He looked at the young man, not knowing what to say. The light was growing a little dimmer and Clyde thought it strange how the lights of the casino reflected off the perspiration on the young man's face.

"You're not in any kind of cahoots like that, are you?" asked the young man. "I mean you're just a driver, right? You're just a regular chauffeur?"

"Yeah," said Clyde. "I'm just a driver waiting to hit Hollywood so I can collect my pay."

"That's good," said the young man. "That's good."

Nothing else was said for quite some time. After a while, Bailey rounded the corner of the Apache and said to Clyde, "Okay, let's go."

Clyde turned on the ignition and swung the car out of the parking lot towards Fremont Street. In the rear view mirror, he saw the young man who said his name was either Charlie Smith or Charlie Bowman – Charlie something – bidding them farewell with a tip of his hat.

"You know him?" asked Bailey.

"Nah," said Clyde. "We were just chewing the fat. We're both chauffeurs. We talked shop for a little."

They filled up with gas at a service station on the outskirts of town and then turned onto Highway 91, heading toward Los Angeles. The sun was setting now, creating at first a pink-tinged sky. In no time it became a blazing fire that spread to every cloud in the west, lighting even the tops of the yuccas on either side of the highway. Bailey crawled over into the back seat and stretched out. Clyde thought he could hear him humming his favorite tune, as he always did.

"Go west, young man," he thought to himself, for he was almost there. He had taken Horace Greeley's advice and had followed the sun. The journey had taken him across mountains and through deserts and petrified forests and across great canyons. And now he was practically there. As he thought ahead to the glorious time when he and Bailey would enter the city of angels and would take in the wonders it held – when he considered all the great opportunities that awaited them there – he clapped his hands in sheer delight. He clapped them together so loudly it should have awakened Bailey. But it didn't; Bailey was sound asleep.

# Chapter 11: Panning for Gold

As Clyde and Bailey were feeling a little tired, and wanted to rest up before they entered Los Angeles, they pulled off the paved road and drove through some brush until they arrived at a spot that both hid the car from the highway and afforded access to a stream. The stream came out of the mountains and wound in and out of a grove of trees as it approached the bend in the highway, ran alongside it for forty yards, and then meandered southward.

Clyde pulled back hard on the emergency brake and then chocked the wheels. After he was sure the car was secure, he reached into the back and threw down their blankets and a tin of coffee.

The very idea that they had stopped in the vicinity of a stream and that they were now in the state of California made Clyde's heart beat a little faster. For like Horatio Alger's characters who rose from rags to riches by dint of sheer hard work and by answering Opportunity when it came knocking, Clyde believed he too could move up in the world through 'luck and pluck;' he believed that if he could apply the latter (which he owned in abundance), the former would carry him upwards.

He listened to the rushing sound of the water as the stream neared the highway and then broke away. He thought he could hear the clicking of pebbles against each other as they trickled downstream, and the tumbling of larger stones, made smoother by the process. And finally, in his mind's eye, he could see among the detritus the rare flash of the tiniest flake of gold appearing, hiding, then reappearing in the gritty water, waiting to be discovered. It had to be so, he thought. But he must not say a word to anyone.

1848 wasn't all that far back. Gold had been discovered at Sutter's Mill in California then. That was known all over the world. The discovery of it had brought on the great Gold Rush, which in turn, had created many rags-to-riches stories almost overnight. Clyde wasn't exactly sure where Sutter's Mill was, but he felt that if so much gold could be found in one area of California, it must exist in other places as well. And even if it had been mined out, thought Clyde, there could be something left over, something missed from all the previous mining, some mineral traces that still trickled down from the hills waiting to be discovered.

He said nothing to Bailey, taking the opportunity instead to set up camp, start supper and smooth out a little place on an overlook where he could later throw down a blanket for a spot to sleep.

Early the next morning, while Bailey slept, Clyde picked up a small shallow pan and headed down the slope towards the stream. He removed his shoes and socks, rolled up his pants legs, and walked out into the cold water. Taking the pan, he bent down and scooped up a handful of gravel, jostled it gently, and looked for anything shiny. He saw nothing. He tossed the dirt out and scooped up another handful. Again he found nothing.

Then he moved over a step or two, and tilted the pan into the fine dark gravel that had collected at the base of a large rock. He lifted the pan and angled it in just such a manner that the force of the stream separated the smaller pebbles from the larger ones. Something in the water flashed and caught Clyde's eye. His heart jumped in his chest. He reached into the pan and picked up a pinch of the fine gravel. Then he moved it around in the palm of his hand, using the tips of his fingers to comb the soil. Not one, but three brilliant metal flakes revealed themselves. He held one up and examined it from different angles in the light and smiled and his conviction overcame his hope that it must be gold.

Looking down, he realized that in his excitement, he had allowed the stream to wash over his trousers, soaking them up to his knees and that at some point, he must have sat down in the icy stream without being aware of it, for his entire backside was wet with mud.

An hour later, Clyde climbed back up the slope toward the camp where Bailey still slept. Once Clyde reached the campsite, he rekindled the fire from the night before and started coffee. In quiet exuberance, he touched his pocket, reassuring himself his found treasure was still there. He had taken his drawstring tobacco pouch and had replaced its contents with a dozen flakes of gold – or what he suspected was gold – and a small nugget a little larger than a pea.

The water in the large tin can boiled vigorously now. Clyde took a handful of ground coffee and tossed it into the boiling water. Then he removed the can from the fire and added a cup of cold water from the stream to settle the grounds. He poured himself and Bailey a cup and sat back on a log to drink it. He furtively patted the drawstring bag inside his trouser pocket and could feel the nugget within. "Pretty damn good coffee," he told Bailey, and thought to himself that it did taste decidedly better that morning.

# Chapter 12: High and Dry in L.A.

On a bright and clear morning in September, Clyde and Bailey entered the outskirts of Los Angeles. It was a day that seemed to be brimming with promise. Everywhere was the din of a modern city bursting at the seams with activity. Businessmen in gray flannel suits glanced sharply at their watches and dashed for bulging streetcars, catching them in the nick of time. And the streetcars clacked and lumbered along the tracks as they carried the workers towards the cluster of multi-storey buildings which was downtown LA. Automobiles congested briefly at intersections and then dispersed; sidewalks throbbed with people two and three abreast walking, hesitating, and dodging their way to a multitude of destinations. Freckle-faced youngsters hawked newspapers from corners.

It was like another world to Clyde. "Looking at all this," he mused, "you'd never have thought there was a Depression at all." He was getting the hang of big city driving now, and told himself there wasn't really much to it. You just had to know where you were going – that was the main thing – and you had to move fast when you got the chance. People weren't real patient in LA, and all the horns seemed to go off at the same time when a light changed from red to green.

Clyde checked his rear-view mirror and maneuvered across two lanes, extending his arm straight out for a left turn. He squeezed in behind another car at the light and waited. Bright sunlight shone through the palms that lined both sides of the street, making Hollywood Boulevard look like a postcard come to life. Clyde drummed his fingers on the steering wheel with his right hand and kept his left out the window. He looked up the boulevard and thought it was Beverly Hills he saw there. The light turned green. Horns honked.

Much later, sitting on the bed in his boarding house room, the thought would occur to Clyde that the bait he dangled out the car window at that fateful moment must have been irresistible. The thought would also occur to him that the cyclist who drifted up behind him on the driver's side, whether a habitual thief or not, probably was unable to pass up the temptation to remove a bracelet watch from the arm of a stranger. The cyclist snatched the watch from Clyde's wrist just as the light turned green and moved on with the flow of the traffic. In the blink of an eye he was gone.

"I'll be damned," said Clyde, looking at the band of pale skin on his wrist where a watch used to be. He changed lanes thinking to follow the thief, but the attempt proved futile. He was soon cut off by other cars and was forced to sit again and wait until the traffic could begin moving again. He looked left and right, then he looked over at Bailey and said, "That was a pretty expensive timepiece."

Bailey just shook his head. "I guess when it rains, it pours," he said.

"What do you mean?" asked Clyde.

"Oh, nothing," said Bailey. He pulled his own timepiece from his pocket, tapped it against the dashboard and glanced at the time.

Once again, traffic started to move. Clyde was taking in famous place names that popped into view – Beverly Hills, Hollywood and Vines – when Bailey said, "Where would you like to go in Hollywood?"

"That one that points the way to Hollywood and Vine," said Clyde. "I've heard a lot about it."

"Hollywood and Vine it is, then," said Bailey. "Take us there." Clyde continued to drive. And as he drove, he was still a little heated about the stolen watch and how easily and quickly it had happened. He felt silly for having such a watch, no matter how smart it looked; he was angry at the thief; he wished he hadn't poked his arm out the window; he wished he hadn't wanted to make a left turn. And in the middle of his thoughts, Bailey said, "Pull over here, Clyde. This is the spot."

Clyde wheeled the car into an empty lot. "Leave her running," said Bailey. "Looks like this is where you'll be getting out. I'll take it from here." The tone of Bailey's voice had changed. There was something of an edge to it now. It wasn't anger or meanness or anything like that, it was just that the old charm that Clyde had become so accustomed to was gone all of a sudden. For a very strange and awkward moment, Clyde thought of the chauffeur in Las Vegas who would give rides to people and let them out in the desert. But it was a silly idea and he banished it from his mind.

"You want me to get out?" he asked Bailey.

"Yep. Take your bags and step out of the car." Clyde reached into the back seat and located first one bag and then the other. He pulled them into the front seat and then stepped out.

"I've got some pay coming," he said to Bailey.

"Well now, Clyde," said Bailey, "I'm sorry about that, but the truth is, I don't have it. These are pretty hard times, as you know. You've been a real good chauffeur and I wish I could pay you what you're worth, but it's just not there. I can give you a couple of dollars for transportation, which doesn't leave me very much, and we can call it even."

He pushed two bills into Clyde's shirt pocket. "Now, if you'll step aside, I need to be moving on."

Clyde stepped aside. He stood in the middle of the vacant lot, holding a bag in each hand while he watched Bailey move into the flow of traffic and turn at the light without even so much as a good-bye or good luck. "Well, how do you like that?" he said. Without knowing exactly where he was headed, and still a little stunned at what had just transpired, he began walking to the end of the block. There was a bus bench there and he sat on it.

Thinking back, Clyde remembered he and Bailey had shaken hands on the deal, but apparently that meant nothing to Bailey. Clyde had pulled him out of the ditch. Clyde had left everything behind to be a chauffeur and go west, and now here he was a month later after Bailey reneged on the agreement and hung him out to dry, standing on the corner of Hollywood and Vine with little more than the clothes on his back and a couple of bucks in his pocket. He wondered if they were counterfeit.

But he had his gold, scant as it was, and he felt sure it was not fool's gold. He walked around Hollywood asking for directions and eventually found a jeweler who offered him cash for the contents of his tobacco pouch. Clyde did pretty well. He now had enough money to pay for a month's stay at a little boarding house. He figured in a month's time he should be able to find a job and support himself.

The owner of the boarding house was a Mrs. Burkett. She was an older lady and nice enough. She wore her gray hair in a loose bun and she was a talker. She talked over her shoulder at him all the way up the stairs as she took him to see his room. She talked about the weather and about her other guests, who were all very nice and she mentioned she hoped Clyde was also a nice man such as they. "They almost all salesmen," she said at the top of the stairs. "Almost to the last man. There's one or two that's not; I'm not sure what their line is, but they pay their rent on time and that's what counts."

Clyde's room was musty but clean, and Mrs. Burkett told him it came with a radio so he could catch up on the news or listen to music at night. "You get two meals a day," she told him. Take your pick which. Most people choose breakfast and dinner. It's up to you."

Clyde thanked Mrs. Burkett and set his bags inside the door. That evening, after supper with the salesmen, he retired to his room, fumbled in his pocket for a pen and began writing a postcard to Zena. It was a modern colored postcard designed to exhibit both the futurism and glamour of Hollywood. On it were palms, luxurious cars and the looming real estate sign on the mountainside shouting to the world that this was Hollywood.

Clyde thought a moment. "Dear Zena," he began. "I'm in Los Angeles now. Things didn't turn out as I expected. That fellow that hired me left me here high and dry. I'll be alright. Love, Clyde."

He removed his shoes, sat on the bed and tuned in a music station on the radio, catching the last verses of a humorous song he had never heard before. The recording was a simple one – vocals and a guitar – about young man who left home and got involved in all sorts of shenanigans and had people tell him fibs and take advantage of him. It occurred to Clyde the song could have been about him. It made him smile. The words of the chorus repeated "Oh, don't you believe it..." and faded into the night.

# Chapter 13: Fuller and RKO

By the end of his first week in LA, Clyde had found employment in two areas, however tenuous those jobs were. On the first day, he had put on his best Sunday clothes, walked to 780 Gower Street in Hollywood, and submitted his application as an extra with RKO Pictures. When he came to the section of the application form titled "previous experience," he wrote that he had busted broncos, dipped sheep, strung fences, built and maintained cars, hired out as a chauffeur, and could probably out hunt and out fish any other applicant RKO had in their files. And with a final flourish, he touched his pencil to his tongue and added that there probably wasn't any kind of work he couldn't do, and do better than anyone else. He then found an official-looking lady dressed in a business suit, and handed her the form as if offering her a gift of great value. She smiled and told Clyde he should check back in a couple of days to see if there were any openings. "That is what I'll do, ma'am," he said and walked out the door.

He felt so good about his prospects he decided to hail a cab instead of walking back to Mrs. Burkett's boarding house. While he rode, Clyde noticed the morning paper left on the seat by the previous passenger. It was folded open to the classified section. In the top right corner, in a sea of tiny agate-type ads – the smallest size the newspaper could set – was a bountiful message set off in large, bold type:

**BE YOUR OWN BOSS!**
**Set Your Own Hours!**
**Take Control of Your Future!**
**You can make up to 55% profit**
**selling over 300 brand-name products**
**to a PRE-SOLD market.**

The signature of the company's founder and president, Alfred C. Fuller, appeared at the bottom of the ad.

Clyde felt it spoke to him personally. He had heard of the company; he had seen its evangelists, carrying their black suitcases door-to-door; and he even knew of one of them at the boarding house who sat at table with him. "This is what I want to do," he thought to himself. "I'll have two jobs here in Los Angeles."

That afternoon, Clyde answered the Fuller Brush ad and had only to await the contract and sales kit that would arrive at the general delivery window of the community post office.

Normally taciturn at the dinner table, Clyde now became suddenly voluble. He wanted to find out all he could about selling the Fuller product line, and sought out Sam, the resident Fuller Brush salesman. Clyde befriended the man, some years his senior, and in the process, told him of his plans to follow the same line of business of selling brushes. While waiting for his own sales kit to arrive by mail, Clyde asked Sam if he could keep him company, "tag along," and learn the ropes, so to speak. "I want to be the best," he told Sam. "I don't want to just make a living; I want to be a success, and I figure I can get a jump on things if I watch you go through your rounds – if you don't mind too much."

"Well, that's okay with me," said Sam. "I wouldn't mind the company, and I'll be glad to show you my techniques, as long as you stay out of my territory and don't end up being my competition." Clyde agreed to that.

After breakfast the next morning, looking very much like the rest of the salesmen, who, after wolfing down buttered biscuits and hot cups of black coffee, were off to the races, Clyde and Sam bade Mrs. Burkett a hasty good morning and were on the way to their route as well.

They took a trolley to a certain part of the city Sam considered his own, and then set out on foot. While they walked, Sam explained the basics to Clyde, often paraphrasing the literature Clyde would soon get with his own sales kit. "If you study Mr. Fuller's life and work philosophy, and take it to heart," said Sam, "you're already pretty much on the road to being a brush salesman. I'll tell you what Mr. Fuller says, and then I'll tell you how I have improved on that with my own methods of getting sales."

"You're going to read how Mr. Fuller came from a family of 12 children and how he believed in hard work, and how he came up picking strawberries for a penny a quart. You're going to read about how he didn't invent brushes – even though some swear he did – but that he improved on them. He talked to hundreds of housewives and maids about what they wanted in a brush. He developed a line of quality brushes that became so popular, he couldn't sell them fast enough. That's where you and I come in, according to Mr. Fuller; for he needs an ever-expanding sales force to deliver his brushes to an eagerly awaiting world." Sam stopped by a fence to tie his shoelace.

"That's what you're going to read," he went on, "but it ain't necessarily so, as the song goes. The brushes don't sell themselves. Sometimes people slam the door in your face, and sometimes they pour water – or worse – on you from the upstairs window."

Then he lowered his voice as the two of them went up the walk to knock on the door of a residence. "I have ways of not only separating them from their hard-earned money, but making them say 'thank you' in the bargain."

Sam rapped smartly on the door. A middle-aged woman wearing an apron appeared, pushing some strands of hair from her eyes. "Excuse me, young lady. Is your mother at home? I have a free sample I would like to give her."

"My mother?" asked the woman. "No. I *am* the mother...I mean, I am the lady of the house. You must mean me."

"Please forgive me, ma'am. You look so young. I am embarrassed to say, I thought you were the daughter. Please accept my apology." Clyde noticed that though he had the lady's attention, he maintained his foot in the door. He held his suitcase at waist level and opened it so that she could see the contents while he looked for the gift he promised to give her.

"These are Fuller Brush Company's finest hog's hair bristle," said Sam, waving his hand over them as he spoke. "I love them! In fact, I believe in them so much, I'm willing to part with a sample for free, just to give people like you the chance to know them as I do. Just decide between the two in my hand, and my partner and I will be on our way." By now the suitcase was completely open, the array of beautiful mahogany-handled brushes of every shape on full display against the black velvet background.

In the end, the lady not took the gift Sam offered, but bought two more. "You have chosen well, ma'am," said Sam. And as he had correctly told Clyde just minutes earlier, the lady thanked them for coming by.

"Do you get the idea?" Sam asked, once he was sure they were out of earshot. Clyde nodded that he did, but that he stopped at telling a grown woman she looked like a young girl.

"I just can't do that," said Clyde. "Why, she'd think I had been out in the sun too long without a hat."

He kept walking with Sam on his route, and stayed with him all day, picking up pointers, taking some to heart and discarding the rest. When the two of them arrived back at the boarding house in time for supper, Mrs. Burkett told Clyde that someone from the "studios" had left a message for him on her house phone to come see them and report in first thing in the morning.

"What does that mean?" she asked him.

"It means they took one look at my application and decided they couldn't take a chance on passing this cowboy up," said Clyde, and he clapped his hands with delight. Mrs. Burkett stared at him blankly, still not seeming to understand.

"It means I got a job with RKO studios, Mrs. Burkett! Who knows where it'll lead? I might even end up in the movies!

R·K·O RADIO
PICTURES Inc.

# Chapter 14: Hollywood Extra

Clyde's first day on the job at RKO studios was nothing like he had expected. He arrived early Tuesday morning, dressed in khaki work clothes and a Stetson hat tilted slightly over and back on his head, looking the very picture of the dashing young, wiry, eager worker ready for anything the company could throw at him. That morning, he had walked the distance to RKO Studios, strode past rows of palms, quick-stepped up to the front entrance of the building, and pushed open the large, polished doors that led into the lobby. Immediately he noticed the difference in the place from the week before. Now there was no sitting room; now people scurried in and out of doors that led to the back; and now there was an air of urgency that seemed to imbue everything – from every word spoken, to every gesture, to every sidelong glance. Clyde stopped someone who looked official and told the man his purpose for being there. That person, in turn, directed him to another person who then processed Clyde's paperwork and ushered him through a pair of large doors. The large doors led into a long hallway and finally into something that resembled an aircraft hangar. It was chaos. People with megaphones barked orders; some carried papers under both arms; while others transported on creaky-wheeled, wobbly carts, assemblies that looked like stage sets. Still others carried bundles of rope, block and tackle, and turned sideways to weave through the crowd.

Clyde saw a man cup his hands to his mouth and shout, "Over here! Set up number three!" From another corner of the hangar a man spoke through a megaphone and said, "Break that set down and move the framework to lot 7!" Just then a worker bumped into Clyde. "You're in the way, pal!" he said, and jostled his way to his destination – somewhere on the far side of the hangar.

The man who brought Clyde into the hangar said, "This is it. This is your job. Report to that man in the vest over there. He'll tell you what to do." He placed a hand on Clyde's back, ready to push him into the fray.

Clyde, still stupefied by the disorganization and frenzied activity inside the hangar, didn't move. "What is this all for?" he asked.

The man looked at him. "You really *don't* know anything, do you?" he said. "It's for that new movie – *Bird of Paradise.* The Studio just signed for it – big production, lots of stars." He opened both hands wide and wiggled them in front of his face. "Hooplah!" Then he pointed again to the man in the vest. "They're waiting for you over there. Go."

And Clyde did as he was told, and went.

There wasn't much to the work, once Clyde found out what was expected of him. In fact, it was easy. He was a glorified mover. He would help break down a set, or transport it, or set it up. He moved fake walls and furniture and mid-sized palm trees. He worked furiously, and then he would sit and wait. Sometimes the waits were just breathers, and other times they were quite long.

And even though he was paid for doing nothing at all during the long waits, Clyde hated being idle. He bought a guitar at a pawnshop and during the long spells of inactivity on the job, he taught himself to play. He plunked at songs he knew, and songs he liked, and tried to reproduce them with the guitar. One of those songs was one he had heard on the radio, "Don't You Believe It," which he was able to learn by heart, and which he often told people who asked to hear it, was a song about his life – about a young man who wanted to fly from home in search of the big world, and how he was tricked and mistreated and forsaken.

He saw several movie actors during his work as an extra, and some he met face-to-face. He had a beer with Joel McCrea and thought him a" pretty good guy, not stuck on himself, but down to earth – one of the boys." Joel McCrea was the leading man in *Bird of Paradise.* He played opposite a dark-haired, big-eyed woman of devastating beauty named Dolores Del Rio whom Clyde had never as yet met. He had read about her in *Variety,* and he had heard others talk about her, but he had never seen her in person. He had read David O.Selznik's famous comment in *Variety,* "I want Del Rio in a love story in the South Seas. I don't care the script, but in the end, Del Rio should be thrown into a volcano," which had made Clyde want to meet her all the more.

While on the set in November, he did meet her. He and some other extras had been called to be part of a crowd scene and stand in as "warm bodies" and they were milling about, waiting to take their places when Clyde heard a megaphone-enhanced voice boom out, "Quiet on the set! Mrs. Del Rio…" It was spoken as if in court, announcing the entrance of the judge and the attending silence and respect his office demanded. And the surrounding crowd did indeed grow quiet. Clyde saw, appearing through a wall of lights, a statuesque woman in a white two-piece bathing suit. She had black, shoulder-length hair and large eyes. She smiled. Someone near him whispered, “Dolores Del Rio!”

As Clyde watched her enter the set and take her place opposite Joel McCrea, he couldn’t take his eyes from her. She was, he thought, simply the most beautiful woman he had ever seen.

# Chapter 15: A Homespun Speech

In 1919, evangelist Billy Sunday declared, "Prohibition is won; now for tobacco." Yet, eleven years later, cigarette consumption in America was 1,500 per capita – the highest it had ever been. Tobacco companies sold 113 billion packets a year. Celebrities such as Al Jolson, Red Skelton and King Vidor endorsed cigarettes, parroting such catch phrases as, "Fresh as May," "Not a cough in a carload," or "Camel: smoke as many as you want; they never get on your nerves."

In the Hollywood circles Clyde frequented, it seemed everyone smoked, and in truth, about half did. Clyde smoked too. He smoked Raleighs, the cigarette that rewarded you with two redeemable coupons tucked inside every packet. If you saved enough coupons, you could have your pick of such attractive gifts as tool kits, camping gear, furniture, and luxury items.

So Clyde began saving his coupons, keeping open his options about which item he should redeem them for. Whatever it was, he was sure, it would be a dilly. He sent off for the Raleigh coupon catalog in the mail. And as he awaited its arrival, his coupon collection, like his habit, continued to grow. He filled first one cigar box and then a second, and kept them hidden under his bed.

He moved from Mrs. Burkett's boarding house into a duplex closer to the movie studios. He could now walk to work in half an hour. The problem was, work was starting to dry up. The production of *Bird of Paradise* had ground on for over a year. Of late, he seldom worked full days. Sometimes he would arrive at the set only to be furloughed after a couple of hours' work. The furlough might last for days or weeks, depending on the production schedule. For the same pay as a stage hand (because in the minds of the producers, it all fell under the umbrella of 'movie extra,'), he was occasionally asked to stand in the background – along with the rest of the crowd, milling about and busying himself with some imaginary purpose. Years later, he would wink in reply to anyone who asked if he had ever acted in the movies, that he had done so, but that some of his best work lay on the cutting room floor.

Clyde often saw Joel McCrae on the set, a few minor actors, and of course the director, King Vidor, but sightings of Mrs. Del Rio were rare. When Clyde worked, he worked hard; and during free time he practiced roping or playing the guitar. When he was off work, he sold Fuller Brushes.

He developed a sales technique so successful that it attracted the attention of the company bigwigs back in Hartford, Connecticut. His success at selling brushes threw him into a limelight far different from the one he had secretly hoped for in the movie industry. In the first place, he didn't mind walking in order to sell his product. He had come into L.A. from the craggy land of the Chisos where walking great distances was commonplace. Once he started selling, Clyde found he could easily cover ten miles a day.

As his mentor Sam had warned him, he encountered the door slammed in the face and the occasional pan of wash water thrown on him from an upstairs window, but he didn't let a few disgruntled people deter or discourage him. "It's like the guy standing on the corner," he would explain. "If he asks every pretty girl that walks by if he can have a kiss, he might get slapped a lot, but sooner or later one of them will say 'yes.' And besides, I never got wet selling brushes – I'm quick as a cat and know to get out of the way of falling water."

He wore a suit and tie on his route (because Mr. Fuller said people respected you in a suit and tie), and crisscrossed L.A. from its ritziest neighborhoods to the seedy underbelly of the city in search of sales. His efforts were rewarded – or at least, acknowledged – in the spring of the following year, when he was named one of the top salesmen in the L.A. area. An awards banquet was to be held in a downtown hotel to honor Clyde and the other sales leaders.

He accepted the invitation and arrived at the banquet dressed in his Sunday best, expecting to nod politely whenever his name was called, but not expecting to give a speech. He had never given a speech – to anyone at any time in his life – unless you considered the time he had to stand up in Mr. Smith's algebra class in high school and explain the commutative property, and even that had given him the cottonmouth and filled him with dread.

So with thoughts of a perfectly enjoyable evening, he walked into the banquet hall and looked all around. It was laid out very nicely. Colored crepe-paper stringers hung in loops from the corners. Dozens of tables, evenly spaced, draped in fresh white linen cloths, took up the largest area of the room. On a higher level, facing the tables was a speaker's platform, a large Fuller Brush banner hanging from the rafters, and a polished wood lectern.

A man in a suit appeared seemingly from out of nowhere and showed Clyde to his table. Clyde saw his name there on a table tent, along with those of three other salesmen. One after another, the other salesmen arrived and took their seats. Clyde made small talk with them, fiddled with his napkin, first unfolding it and placing it on his lap, and then removing it, only to place it back on his lap again. He pulled a timepiece from his pants pocket and checked the time.

The meeting began promptly at 8 o'clock. Clyde and the others listened as first one person and then another approached the dais and either introduced someone or delivered a terse little speech. Somewhere in the middle of the banquet, a man on the platform said, “And now we would like to acknowledge one of our top sales leaders in the Los Angeles area, Clyde Whistler.” The speaker looked about the room for a moment, found Clyde in the crowd, and gestured towards him. There was applause. Clyde half stood up, smiled, nodded, and then sat back down.

“Won’t you come up and say a few words, Clyde?” continued the speaker.

“Speech!” Clyde heard some troublemaker say from across the room. Then a couple of the people from his own table said, “Speech!” Another person pushed Clyde from his chair, and he had no choice but to go.

Amid the diminishing cries of ‘speech,’ Clyde made his way to the platform, and then to the lectern, where the speaker shook his hand, and turned the floor over to him.

Clyde felt he must have looked red-faced as he stood there facing the room of over a hundred people. He swallowed, took a deep breath, and smiled, secretly afraid of hearing the first few sounds of his own voice. Finally he spoke. “I’m a cowboy,” he said quite loudly, “from the good ol’ state of Texas!” The people at the tables laughed, then applauded.

To Clyde’s surprise, he was able to speak with less pain and effort after the applause. He lost the jitters and his knees stopped knocking. The thought occurred to him to look upon the crowd as if he were talking any of the hundreds of strangers to whom he had sold brushes on his route.

“I have been honored at this banquet for selling a lot of brushes. If people want to know my secret,” he said, wiping his sleeve on his forehead, “there really isn’t one. I make a lot of sales because I treat everyone I come across like they were a friend of mine, and I’m just offering them a little advice, just like I would a friend. I might say, ‘you work hard in this house, ma’am, and it shows.” His voice took a hint of melody as he related his technique.” This brush will make your work go a lot easier...it’s the best brush made. It is pure hog’s hair bristle.’” He shrugged his shoulders. “And it goes from there,” he continued. “If she says ‘no,’ it’s not the end of the world. After all, I’m just a friend offering a little advice. More often than not, though, she’ll buy a brush from me. It’s all in being honest and how you treat your customers.”

At that point in his speech, Clyde didn’t know how much time had passed – whether he had spoken for one minute or fifteen. He thought he probably should wrap it up and sit down, but he couldn’t resist the temptation to tell them all a joke. “I started out by telling you that I was a cowboy from Texas,” he said. “There’s the story about an artist, a preacher and a cowboy who came up on the edge of the Grand Canyon and were standing there, looking down at the miles of sculpted rock towers and awe-inspiring cliffs. The artist said as how it would be such a beautiful picture to paint, then the preacher said it was a wonderful example of God’s handiwork, and how beautiful and gorgeous it was. When it came the cowboy's turn, he removed his hat, looked down into the canyon and said, 'Damn! I'd sure hate to lose a cow down there.'"

Clyde heard ripples of laughter. He went on a while longer, thanking the people who invited him to the banquet, and for the excellent meal – even though he hadn't as yet had a chance to sample it. And then he said, "That's about all I've got to say. Thank you."

Later in the evening, long after the laughter and the applause had ended, he weighed the situation and came to the conclusion that he hadn't done too badly his first time up. He had entertained them. He had made them laugh. But it had been a nightmarish experience. He had been as scared as he remembered being in a long time, and he knew he never wanted to stand up in front of a bunch of strangers and give a speech again.

# Chapter 16: The Cast Party

In the spring of 1935, after a series of fits and starts, the production of *Bird of Paradise* was drawing to an end. Customarily, cast parties followed the end of a film's production; and it was usually a time for all the participant in the film to let their hair down a little. It was a time of revelry, toasts, and of congratulations. It was also the singular event many of the cast anticipated most. Dolores del Rio, thankful not only to her supporting cast and crew, was more thankful the filming was finished. She was determined her cast party was going to be one for the books. She pressed King Vidor and the producers for an extravaganza that would go beyond what had been done in the past. It would be open to all who had been involved in carrying the film through to its conclusion – everyone from secretaries to key grips, extras and stage hands. There would be bright lights and hors-d'oeuvres and wall-to-wall food and drinks and of course, dancing to the music of a big name band. It would be a personal expression of Mrs. Del Rio's gratitude, and it would be an event to remember for years to come.

Clyde received his invitation and immediately began making mental preparations for it: whether he would wear his dress boots and hat; whether he would wear the same suit and tie he had worn to the Fuller Brush banquet, and whether he would invite a lady friend. As he was making preparations, he received a post card from Zena telling him to "get ready", that she and Buster were coming to L.A. to see him.

Zena had married Buster in 1926. Buster rode bulls in rodeos for prize money until too many injuries forced him into another line of work – rodeo clown. He turned out to be quite successful at it. His act included a clever mule named Dutch whom Buster would put through the paces. Buster would wear one of Zena's dresses and sashay into the arena, his eyes barely visible under a red wig and turban. Then he would climb onto Dutch backwards, tumble off unceremoniously, jump to his feet, hike up his dress, and repeat the absurdity all over again. One slapstick farce would follow the other, culminating with Buster and Dutch jumping over a toy car. Afterwards, he would pretend to lose Dutch, who would be standing right behind him; then Buster would whistle for the animal, only to have Dutch poke his huge head under Buster's arm.

The crowd had loved it, both Buster's madcap zaniness, and the antics and savoir-faire of the lovable mule Dutch. The act became a living for Buster and Zena as they attached it to the rodeo and played it out in city after city, following the circuit from Tulsa, Oklahoma to Madison Square Gardens; and from Boston

Gardens to Los Angeles. Since they didn't own an automobile, they hitched rides from whomever and wherever they could get them.

And in the spring of 1935, their act was taking them to L.A., where they were to take part in the annual rodeo. The first thought into Clyde's mind on receiving the news was that they would be his guests at the cast party. And so they were. Clyde dismissed from his mind any ideas of bringing a lady friend. Everything else happened according to schedule.

On the appointed night, Clyde, Zena and Buster dressed in proper evening attire and took a cab to RKO. Once there, they climbed the stairs to the entrance way where they were momentarily detained by an RKO attendant. He checked Clyde's ID, took note of his guests, and then pointed them toward the large doors behind him. The three of them passed through the doors and walked for a bit, Clyde and Buster's steel-tipped shoes clicking as they did so. They walked down hallways and around corners, proceeding for what seemed like miles, until they were met by the sounds of party and celebration.

Clyde wasn't sure if they had walked under a waterfall or were in the middle of an auditorium full of honking geese. There was a band playing and so many people talking that he could hardly hear what Zena and Buster were saying. Multi-colored stringers crisscrossed the same room where Clyde had spent over a year previously, putting together and knocking down sets, answering cattle calls for stand-ins and warm bodies, and even practicing guitar during times of inactivity. He had spent almost as much time here as he spent at home. It had been his workplace. Now, it was wall-to-wall people – many of whom he knew. Waiters seemed to be at every turn. They balanced trays of drinks and *hors-d'oeuvres* and threaded their way through the crowd and back again. Clyde took a drink and a little piece of beef and cheese on a toothpick and looked over at Zena. "Ain't this sumpin'?" he practically shouted, but she couldn't hear him. She just smiled back.

At one end of the room was a bandstand. Musicians in tuxedos played popular tunes to a packed and energetic group of dancers. And then, entering the room as she had the first time he saw her, walking through a wall of lights, Clyde saw Dolores del Rio. Attendants were on either side. As had happened the first time, the crowd hushed. Someone said, "Dolores del Rio," and almost at the same time, another person echoed the remark.

She was as beautiful as ever, Clyde thought. She shook a few hands, exchanged remarks and made her way across the room. Buster knew who she was. He nudged Clyde. "The next dance, why don't you ask her?" he said. "You ought to."

The thought petrified Clyde. In spite of himself, he told Buster he would.

Mrs. Del Rio was still making her way through the crowd. Clyde could see her greet each new person and could practically hear her thank them for their hard work on the movie. Just then, the bandleader struck the music stand with his baton and raised his arms to begin the next tune. Mrs. Del Rio was standing directly in front of Clyde now, smiling her gorgeous smile. Buster nudged him hard in the ribs and whispered, out of sight to Mrs. Del Rio, "Ask her!"

"Mrs. Del Rio," Clyde began, reaching to shake her hand.

"Yes?" she said.

"I'm a great admirer of yours. I have...I have always liked..." Clyde felt Buster nudge him hard in the ribs, and he broke off his sentence to start anew. His heart was pounding. His face was red. He started to say, "May I have this dance?" and the phrase was right there on the tip of his tongue, but no sound came forth. She continued to stand before him, waiting to hear what he would say. Just then another movie extra in a nice suit cut in and said, "Mrs. Del Rio, may I have this dance?" She nodded and the two of them spun off across the dance floor, in perfect time with the music.

Buster and Zena danced and enjoyed the music and the evening. Later, before Mrs. Del Rio wished them all the best and disappeared into the night, Buster asked her to dance and she accepted. He smiled over his shoulder at Clyde during one of the turns and bowed gallantly at the end of the dance.

As often as the story would come up later in their lives, Buster liked to remind Clyde of the party (much to Clyde's chagrin) and needle him that "faint heart never won fair maid."

As for Buster and the rodeo act, it came to an abrupt end when he lost Dutch to the lure of the wild. One summer evening in Sierra Blanca, Texas, Dutch escaped her pen, even under Zena's watchful eye, and was never seen or heard from again.

# Chapter 17: The Rabbit Skin Coat

In the summer of 1935, Clyde, whose accumulation of Raleigh coupons had born witness to an ever-increasing cigarette habit, met and fell desperately in love with a young lady who (to Clyde at least) embodied a popular Depression-era tobacco slogan: "As fresh as May." Her name was Dorothy. She had wavy, light brown hair that reflected blonde in sunlight and bounced from her shoulders as she walked. She was wasp-waisted and preferred to dress in Western cowgirl attire, accentuating her figure with lightly starched, pressed Levi's. She had a few freckles across her nose, appearing more as beauty marks than blemishes and she possessed flirtatious brown eyes as sparkling and surprising as her personality.

Everything about Dorothy – from her calico blouse to her cinch belt to her boots – reminded Clyde of home and the people and the land he had forsaken for his journey west. Almost as a knee-jerk reaction, he determined not to forsake her as well. He would do everything in his power to keep her; he would woo and serenade her. His friends and acquaintances would notice the spring in Clyde's step and his inability to focus on anything in his path but Dorothy, and would come to the same conclusion: he was smitten.

Clyde had met and dated others before Dorothy, but none of those ladies had come close to her good looks and personality. The most recent had been the young lady Clyde had met while on the movie set – slim and comely and someone whose company he thought he might enjoy – but she torpedoed any possibility of a future relationship the night of their first date when the two of them were making small talk and Clyde, after considering for a moment her last name, told her he thought he knew her daddy. "Oh, that old drunk?" she asked with a scowl.

"I didn't have anything to do with her after that," Clyde later said. "And I never asked her out again. Imagine a woman who doesn't have any more respect for her father than that!"

He had met other women on and off the set, but their relationships too had been short-lived. It was Dorothy he now thought of night and day. The two of them seemed so well matched, at least in Clyde's mind. They did the things dating couples did in LA. They attended movies, had picnics in the park, and showed up at dances where they danced until the place closed. Clyde entertained her with his guitar, plunking away at popular songs and finishing with his personal favorite, "Don't You Believe It," which always made Dorothy laugh.

On several occasions he dropped hints that when Christmas rolled around, he would have something special for her, something she – or any woman for that matter – would really like. And then he would go home and take out his boxes of coupons from under his bed, count them, and pore over the Raleigh Tobacco catalog to see what he could redeem them for. He was narrowing down all his options to a fur coat. When he opened the dog-eared catalog to the coat, it stood out large on the page. It may have been dyed rabbit skin, but it looked extremely smart, almost like a mink stole. He angled the catalog away from him and shifted the image in the glare of the naked bulb at his bedside in order to get a better look. He wished he could heft it in his hands and feel its weight and see it from all sides as it really was, and not just a photograph.

And maybe soon he would. In the moments when he wasn't thinking about the things that made up his day-to-day life, and about making a living, he would lapse back to the coat and, like a word problem in a math class back in school, calculate precisely how many cigarette packages he had to smoke before he could own the fur coat. And every time he completed the word problem, his calculations took him to the same point: Christmastime. Good then. That is what he would do. Dorothy would be so surprised, and in the middle of the Depression when really nice things were hard to come by.

In the meantime, his work as a movie extra dried up. After *Bird of Paradise* left town, he was unable to find work as an extra in any of the other studios. In addition, his Fuller brush sales were dropping off. Clyde was now just maintaining his client base without adding any new ones, and he supposed what he needed was to venture into new territory. But he wouldn't do that. He wouldn't undertake any activity that would remove him farther from Dorothy. She was here and near him and in his life. He didn't want to be anywhere else.

Summer came and went. Towards the end, on his birthday, Dorothy baked him a chocolate cake, his favorite. It was topped with 24 candles. She had invited their mutual friends, some from her neighborhood and some from RKO studios, and together they sang 'happy birthday' to Clyde. It was a Monday, and a day and time he would not likely forget. There had been a light mist in the early morning, and Clyde had beheld from the rolled-down window of the taxicab a double rainbow in the sky. He took it as a good omen. TIME Magazine hit the newsstands that morning with a full-length shot of the actress Jean Harlow on the cover of Time Magazine; the airwaves were flooded with the sounds of "It's Love, Baby," by Louis Brooks and his Hi-Toppers; and a daring and congenial Amelia Earhart had begun her flight to Hawaii from the mainland. For Clyde, it had been a happy birthday indeed. He felt good about things. He was young and strong, had the girl of his dreams in his corner, and almost had the world by the tail. Well, he may have loosened his grip on the tail at times, but success was in sight – he was sure of that.

By October he could wait no longer. He gathered all the cigarette coupons he had and sat until late in the night separating them into envelopes of twenty. He sealed the envelopes and wrote the number count on the back of each. Then he neatly pushed them all into a much larger envelope and enclosed a check to make up for the coupons he lacked. The next morning, Clyde carried his bundle to the post office. Within the bundle he had enclosed a check and a note explaining that he hoped it would make up the difference he owed. He was fairly certain the Raleigh people would accept it and send him the coat.

Weeks passed. Time crept along excruciatingly slowly with each new day posting the same results: no package, no coat. Clyde wondered if he had been played the fool. He wondered if all this talk about a tobacco company redeeming coupons was just so much smoke and nonsense. And the more he thought about it, the more it ate at him that he had (in a moment of unclear thought) actually sent money to a cigarette company.

And just when he was on the verge of writing the company a letter, he got a notice from the post office that a package was waiting for him in general delivery. As if by magic, every nagging, gnawing doubt and misgiving had turned to euphoria.

The next day, Clyde picked up his package, brought it back to his flat and opened it. The coat had the smell of fresh-tanned leather. It had a silk lining, a single-piece fur collar and sleeves and lush, thick fur pelts running lengthwise down the coat. He thought how beautiful Dorothy would look in this. He would have to take her to a nice place where she could show it off.

The following Friday, he arrived at Dorothy's home. He dressed as he always did for their Friday evening dates. He was fresh-shaven, splashed with *Old Spice* and his thick brown hair was oiled with hair tonic and trained almost straight back. He carried the fur coat in a box under his right arm and tapped the doorknocker with his left.

Then it happened: things went south. From the moment she opened the door, Clyde noticed that somehow things had changed between them. She seemed cool and distant. But he paid his observations no mind. He was too happy to see her and bursting at the seams to hand her the coat. He asked if he might come in; and she glanced down at the package he carried under his arm. Then she stood aside to allow him to enter.

Once inside, they sat opposite each other, he on the sofa and she on a chair; he nervous and excited, she preoccupied and distracted by something else. The thought shot across his mind that someone might have died, but he pushed it aside, being able only to think about the fur coat. Nervously, he removed the box from under his arm and practically blurted out, "I have a surprise for you."

"Oh?" she said.

"Well, maybe it's not really that much of a surprise, since I've been hinting around about it for a good long time now, but I'll bet it's nothing you imagined." He handed the box to her. "Open it," he said.

She did. The bow slipped to the floor and the loosely wrapped paper fell away. She lifted the coat out of the box and stood up, allowing it to reach its full length. "This is beautiful, Clyde," she said. "It's just gorgeous!" She ran her hand over the sleeves and the front of the coat. She held it to her shoulders in front of the mirror and didn't say much for a long time.

"It just makes what I have to say to you that much more difficult," she said at last. She fumbled for words and lost them. She started her sentences several times, not really saying anything Clyde could follow. He was puzzled.

She tried again. "I've been thinking about you and me a lot lately," she said. She paused long. "I don't think this is working out. I don't think we should see each other anymore."

Clyde was dumbstruck.

Dorothy continued, changing the tone of her voice from cool to cold. "And now that I've said my piece," she said, "I'd like you to leave."

Clyde remembered thinking that he had been kicked by mules that hadn't hurt as badly as her few words did. And at that moment, he much preferred the kick of the mule. He tried to muster some sort of response, but couldn't. No words came. He was confused, dazed, and hurt. He stood up and turned away from her.

"Close the door on your way out," she said. "And thanks for the coat. It is beautiful."

He imagined she smiled as she spoke the last part, but he didn't really know, because he didn't see her face. He closed the door behind him.

Outside, the autumn air felt cool on his cheeks. He walked towards his flat, his hands in his pockets. For a reason he couldn't explain, he thought of the painting of the wolf that stood over his mother's bed back home and how it looked down on the little ranch house in the snow and how lonely the wolf looked as it breathed steam into the cold winter air. He remembered what Biggun said, that she liked the painting because it made her feel cold. And all of a sudden Clyde felt overtaken with sadness and nostalgia. The images of his mother raced through his mind. He could hear her voice and he missed her. He missed his dad and all his comic quirkiness. He missed the ranch and the Big Bend and everything in between.

Clyde quickened his pace. Like the winter wolf in the painting, he breathed steam into the air. "I'm leaving here," he said. "I'm heading home."

# Chapter 18: Working for the Queen

Feeling lonely and bitter, in a time of year usually given over to feelings of reunion of kith and kin, Clyde culled his belongings into those necessary things that could fit in a single suitcase, walked to a main thoroughfare and put out his thumb, hoping for a ride to Las Vegas and eventually back to Texas. He got rides from nice people, and from curious people, and from people just wanting some company as they drove the highways. It took him several rides to get as far as Bisbee, Arizona, and there his journey stalled. The man Clyde was riding with was turning north from Bisbee, but told Clyde he could take him to the edge of town where he stood a better chance of catching another ride.

Clyde was a little weary and in want of a change of clothes and a good night's sleep. He thought the picturesque little town was as good a place as any. "No," he told the man. "Just drop me off downtown. That'll be fine with me." He then thanked the stranger for his generosity and stepped out of the car with his suitcase.

He had driven through Bisbee with Jack Bailey on the way to California and although his first visual encounter with the little town had been more like a snapshot, briefly perceived through sleepy eyes, it appeared to him much like a Hollywood movie set: perfect, iconic, and with not an element out of place – not a tin can, a herringbone hat, a walking cane, a young lady with expertly upswept hair, sitting on a veranda of a clapboard house behind a white picket fence, nor the slow swoosh of a late model automobile passing under a tree-lined avenue.

Maybe, Clyde thought, he could stay here for a night or so – long enough to take in the town – and throw off the bad memories and feelings he had carried with him ever since leaving LA.

He stayed for more than a night; he ended up spending almost a year in Bisbee. It was a friendly town, very much alive and bustling with activity. The new railroad, built to transport north a multitude of ore, but mainly copper, also brought in fresh foods and the latest clothing accessories from Chicogo, making it possible for the denizens to enjoy oysters on the half shell in the tonier restaurants and shop for bowler hats and three-piece suits in the clothing stores on Main Street.

The open and friendly community of Bisbee was much to Clyde's liking. He set up residence in a local boarding house and began the new year by finding employment with the Copper Queen Consolidated Mining Company in January of 1936. It would be a year marked by milestones in technology, sports and entertainment; but it would also sound the rumblings of another Great War.

When Clyde first entered the mines and began shoveling ore for a living, Benny Goodman & Orchestra were recording "Stompin' and the Savoy" on Victor Records. In the daily papers, Clyde would notice two new newcomer cartoons: *Felix the Cat* and *The Phantom.* And when he listened to the radio after supper, he would chuckle at the comedy of Edgar Bergen and his dummy Charlie McCarthy, unsure, as most of the audience was, which was the dummy.

Later in 1936, Joe DiMaggio would emerge on the sports scene as a new giant in the baseball world. Joe Louis, the boxer who converted a brutal contest of fisticuffs into 'scientific boxing,' fell to the piston-like blows of the German Max Schmeling. And still later in the year, the great Jesse Owens set the 100-meter record of 10.2 seconds.

The year 1936 seemed to be one bursting with energy, growth and innovation. In November, FDR won his second election in a landslide; Chancellor Hitler brazenly sent troops into the Rhineland, used his new Luftwaffe to bomb Madrid in support of Generalissimo Francisco Franco, and signed the Anti-Kommintern Pact with Japan.

The Chinese wish or curse, "may you live in interesting times," held true for Clyde in the year 1936. The ease with which he secured a job in the mines seemed to be an indicator that the economy was possibly turning around -- at last -- and that work, in general, was becoming more plentiful. All Clyde had to do was show up, and he was hired by the greatest employer in the area, the Copper Queen Consolidated Mining Company. He didn't have to sell himself and his skills, as he had in Hollywood; there was a minimal amount of paperwork, and he was sent to work almost as soon as he had put the signing pen back in its holder.

Clyde had never been afraid of hard work, but this was one time he wished he hadn't been so quick to accept employment. Working for "The Queen," he soon discovered, was backbreaking and almost too much for a man, even a healthy young one. Clyde was taken down to the bottom floor of the mine where he was ushered into one of the chambers. It was illuminated by bright lights on poles and loosely strung across the ceiling. The chamber was hot and humid. As people moved about, the lights cast larger-than-human shadows on the walls.

As Clyde surveyed his quarters, his eyes falling first on the string of ore cars and then on the mounds of ore, on the tracks that carried the carts, approaching out of darkness into the starkly lit chamber, and then returning to darkness, he was surprised to find himself staring into the unfriendly eyes of someone who could only have been the shaft foreman.

The foreman was holding out a shovel to Clyde. "Here," he said, pointing to the mounds of ore. The shovel was large and deeply scooped. After the foreman told

Clyde his job was to load the ore cars as they came down the track, it seemed every other statement out of the man's mouth ended with the word "fired." Clyde was be told if he slacked, he was fired; if he failed to meet his quota, he was fired; if he failed to show up to work on time, he was fired. Clyde considered the man's words and then set to work.

Many times that day, he thought he would die. The cars demanded to be filled. They lurched and clanked past him in an unending file; there was no rest between filling one up and starting the next. He pushed himself and his muscles ached. Sometimes he felt he could hardly stand. He didn't know how, but he managed to put in his eight hours. Then he went home, ate and fell into bed. The next day, the process started all over again.

Not long after he had been employed, a foreman came to Clyde and told him he needed an air bender. "What's it look like?" asked Clyde, and was told it was metallic and rubbery and shiny and that it was needed right away and to go looking for it.

Clyde recognized the joke. "Sure thing, Boss!" he said. Then he went back to an isolated part of the mine, crawled up among the rocks and went to sleep. He slept until noon. He re-emerged, saw the Big Boss and told him he had been sent to look for an air bender, but had failed to find one. The Big Boss stormed off and chewed the foreman out for wasting the Company's time.

Another time, Clyde saw a man who had slipped and fallen into a pit, dead. The memory of the sight haunted him. He realized then how dangerous work in the mine could be.

In time, however, Clyde grew accustomed to the work. He took pride in the fact he had survived a month in Hell, living and working in the bowels of the earth. The pay he received was fair, and soon he was able to not only pay his necessities, but to buy some luxury items and treat himself to an occasional night on the town as well.

With every new woman he danced with on the Arizona border, he told himself he was slowly getting over Dorothy in Los Angeles.

On one of his nights out, he bumped into a firecracker of a lady, someone with boundless energy who seemed always to be smiling, laughing and fun loving, and who, more than anything else, loved to dance. She soon persuaded Clyde to take her to dance bars on the Mexican side of the border because everything was cheaper there, especially drinks and entertainment.

She was right. Clyde found he could have a whole lot more fun in Mexico for not much more than a song.

On a Wednesday evening, she asked him to take her across. He did. They had so much fun dancing he lost all sense of time. Looking out a window, Clyde noticed the sky growing lighter in the east. "My, my!" he said, placing his glass on the table. "I've got to be at work in an hour! I don't know where the evening has gone."

Clyde quickly grabbed a cab, took his lady friend across the border and let her off at her house. He hurriedly dressed for work and barely got to the mine in time for work. It was Thursday. Work that day was as strenuous as on any other day, but more difficult for Clyde still, who was going without sleep or rest, or food.

Dog-tired, he trudged home at the end of the workday and found a note attached to his front door. It was from his lady friend and read, "Last night was such fun, Clyde. Let's go back over tonight. Swing by around seven, won't you?"

"Definitely not," Clyde thought. "I need some rest. All I want to do is fall into bed and sleep." He ate a sandwich, sat on the bed and laid his head on his pillow. The ringing of the telephone awakened him. It was his lady friend.

"Clyde," she said, "are you coming by to pick me up?" Tired as he was, he couldn't refuse her.

Once they were across the border, inside the dance hall, dancing, enjoying the almost carnival atmosphere, laughing, drinking, Clyde practically forgot how tired and sleepy he had been earlier. His lady friend was joyous and effervescent as always, as was her fun-loving nature, and Clyde was enjoying every minute spent with her, when an eerie light appeared through one window in the corner of the dance hall: the first orange rays of the morning sun.

He spoke the words, but it was as if someone outside himself was saying them. They sounded distant, as in a dream. "My, my! I've got to be at work in an hour. I don't know where the evening has gone."

As he had done on Thursday, Clyde rushed to work, getting there just in time. He didn't know where he found the energy, but he put in a full day shoveling ore in the chamber of the mine.

At the end of the day, he dragged himself home and fell into bed. The phone rang and rang, or maybe he dreamt it did. In real life, it may have been his lady friend, asking him out on the town once again. Or it could have all been part of a delirious dream, he didn't know. He awoke on Sunday morning, not fully rested in spite of the time spent sleeping, wondering for the third time in three days where the time had gone.

But back home in Texas, a long time ago, hadn't John Whistler chided him for the flaw he perceived in Clyde as a young boy? "Good thing you weren't born a girl," his dad said. "You can't say 'no.'" Clyde's memory of his dad was so sharp he could almost see him in the room of the boarding house, staring at Clyde and shaking his head, exclaiming, "Um-um," under his breath, and then getting up and puttering about the room, examining small items that lay about, such as scissors, needle and thread, pencil and paper on a writing desk.

"Fine fix you got yourself into here, son," Clyde imagined his dad saying. "Going west, young man, like the newspaper man said. Think you'll be coming back home some time?"

Clyde sat on a straight-backed chair in the middle of the room, still feeling the deprivation of going so long without sleep or rest, waiting impatiently for some degree of normalcy to return to his body. His dad's voice echoing in his head, he sat down at the writing desk, wetted the pencil on the tip of his tongue and began a letter to Aunt Esther. She would be the first family member he would meet coming back to Texas.

He announced to her he was coming and that he would be there within a month. He signed the note, 'Love, Clyde,' and sealed it. The next day he resigned his job at the Queen, settled his debts about town, and packed his few belongings to hitch hike back to Texas. He could hardly wait to see the place again.

# Chapter 19: Eve

Eve Avant, the ink on her sheepskin from Draughn's School of Business barely dry, stood alone in the home of her new employer, a Mrs. Willie Jeffers. Mrs. Jeffers had brought Eve to her home, where the two of them had passed first through a carved front door, and then traveled from room to elegant room until they reached the place where Eve now stood. Then Mrs. Jeffers asked Eve to wait a bit whiles he attended to other matters.

Eve waited. It may have been some sort of test, for all she knew. She had heard and read about such things – prospective employers who would leave you alone and watch unawares to see how you behaved when no one was watching you. And in case it was a test, Eve would go along. She stood, hands clasped in front of her. Waiting, not knowing for sure if it would be okay for her to sit, she allowed herself to luxuriate in her surroundings. She let her eyes play about the room, taking in the furnishings one at a time: the full-length drapes; the louvered walls; the mahogany cabinets; a single settee, placed before a window to provide a view of the garden; Louis XIV chests and armoires; and against a far wall, an oversized, gilded mirror also finished in the style of the Sun King. Eve drew near the mirror and beheld herself for a brief time. If only she had a camera to capture the moment: there she stood, dressed in white from her cap to her shoes, her light brown hair pinned perfectly, looking very much the maid in spite of everything her degree had prepared her for. She stood on a Persian rug and stepped back a bit in order to allow more of the rug's design to appear in the mirror. The very moment she took the step, she noticed the rug seemed to float just above the hardwood floor, and she with it. It all seemed to have been torn from the pages of Arabian Nights. It took her breath away. It was magical. Eve remembered thinking on that day that everything in and about the room was new and exciting and magical, and a harbinger of things to come.

This was her first real job since graduating from business school. Her father had approached her every day since her graduation asking, "Well, Eve. Have you found a job yet?" He had been firm and insistent. Now, at last, she was able to tell him she did have a job. It may not have had much to do with her degree, but it was a job, and she had secured it during a period when jobs and money were scarce. At the very least, her resume had impressed Mrs. Jeffers, who was only looking for a caregiver and housekeeper. It was good, Mrs. Jeffers said, that Eve knew typing and dictation and shorthand. It revealed initiative on her part and a sense of discipline that would serve her well in her duties in the Jeffers household.

Mrs. Jeffers was an employer, Eve was to discover, who could exhibit a bit of an edge at times, and certainly demanding, but she wasn't terrible to work for. What impressed Eve was that Mrs. Jeffers was modern, in touch with the times. Not only was her home wired for electricity, but she had lighting in every room. She also had a personal telephone on a stand next to the settee, and in the opposite corner, placed upon a small table, as if it was made for it, looking like a large black honeysuckle blossom on a base, an Electrola gramophone.

Eve was nearing the gramophone when she heard steps. It was Mrs. Jeffers.

"Hello," she said nicely. "I apologize for leaving you here by yourself for so long. I had to attend to some other matters." That was just what she had told Eve half an hour ago, and she still hadn't specified what the 'matters' were.

"Sure enough," said Eve, not quite knowing what else to say.

Mrs. Jeffers then told Eve what she expected from her as far as the job was concerned. Eve would have room and board, and would receive payment every two weeks. For that she was expected to sweep, dust and mop as necessary; to wash, iron and fold linens; and to make the beds. She had kitchen privileges and might, on occasion, be asked to prepare meals. As for the radio and gramophone, she was allowed to play them while Mrs. Jeffers was away – not while she was home.

"Do you think you can abide by everything I've told you?" asked Mrs. Jeffers.

"Yes ma'am. I believe I can," said Eve.

"Good!" said Mrs. Jeffers. "Let's get started, then. You may go from the front of the house to the back, cleaning and straightening as you go. Do it all in your own good time. You'll see what needs doing; when you do, take care of it. I'll need you to pick up in the antechamber and wash the clothes piled up in the hamper in the back."

"Yes ma'am," said Eve, drawing tight her apron.

"But first of all – "Mrs. Jeffers said. "The very first of all, I would like you to spruce up the kitchen and dining rooms and get out the silver and put down that new table cloth. I have a nephew, Clyde...he's been out west for years now...out in California. He sent word that he's coming into town tomorrow for a visit. I want to do the place up nice for him."

Mrs. Jeffers left the room, and perhaps the house. Eve wasn't sure. She busied herself at nothing much at all, thinking, mostly. When she heard Mrs. Jeffers' car start up and pull out of the driveway, Eve turned a knob on the radio and heard the muffled 'pop' as it warmed up. She made her way to the dining room to begin her cleaning there, as Mrs. Jeffers had asked. It wasn't in such bad shape. Eve had seen worse – a paper or two out of place, chairs pulled out from the table. This job wouldn't be that bad, she thought. She dusted the table and centerpiece and was looking to see where Mrs. Jeffers kept her silverware when a song came crackling over the radio, *Bei Mir Bist Du Schoen*, by the Andrews Sisters.

As she worked, she sang along with the Andrews Sisters. The song cheered her -- partly because it was "the latest" on the charts; partly because it was a beautiful harmony; and partly because Eve knew the words in German. Then the song faded to an end and there was nothing but dead air on the radio.

"Clyde?" Eve asked herself. "What kind of name is that?"

# Chapter 20: A Whirlwind Romance

Clyde had been in a good mood ever since crossing the border into Texas. He had traveled through the Franklin Mountains to the booming border town many still referred to as "El Paso del Norte," dipped down into Sierra Blanca and the Davis Mountains, and then even farther south to the Big Bend. Here he was in the familiar haunts of his youth. Everything now seemed more expansive, more hopeful and more optimistic. He had the surprising sensation he could breathe again.

He wanted to kiss the ground he stood on, or to hug it at least, but thought better of doing so. Uncle Terry and Aunt Esther would be overjoyed to see him, and he them. He would drop by their ranch for a spell, and then move on to Sanderson and Del Rio, where he would see first his folks and then Aunt Willie. Maybe, it occurred to him, he could find work in Del Rio. He could do anything; he had chauffeured and acted and shoveled ore; he had lived off the land when he had to, and in the big city when he didn't. He had dealt with scoundrels and rogues and had rubbed elbows with the famous and the beautiful. What couldn't he now do?

It was mid-August when he reached Aunt Willie's. With his hair just cut and oiled, his shirt ironed and his slacks creased, Clyde bounded up the stairs of Aunt Willie's house and rapped sharply at the front door, an expectant smile on his face. He wondered what she would think of him after so much time away, if she would find that all the travails he had endured in the intervening years had in some way changed him.

The thought crossed his mind that for once he was not knocking on a door with a suitcase of Fuller brushes in one hand, waiting to see the lady of the house, and he almost chuckled out loud at the thought. He turned the back of his hand to knock again. But just then, the door opened.

A stranger, and not at all his Aunt Willie, stood in the doorway before him. She was a young woman – a strikingly pretty, statuesque young woman – dressed all in white. He remembered telling Zena later that at the moment of their meeting, he thought he had seen an angel.

He asked who she was, and she gave her name as "Eve." She told him she was the housekeeper and that Mrs. Jeffers had sent her to get the door, and that she presumed he was Mrs. Jeffers' nephew Clyde.

"That I am," said Clyde.

That meeting spawned a series of anecdotes and a whirlwind romance. Clyde remembered very little of his visit to Aunt Willie's, except for any part of it that concerned her attractive housekeeper, Eve. The next day he asked Eve on a date and she, a little surprised at his boldness, accepted. The two of them hit it off very well. On their first date Clyde took Eve across the river into Mexico where they dined and danced, and talked and laughed, and bought serapes and maracas in the sunny open market. A street photographer took their picture.

Within a week's time, Clyde asked Eve to marry him. She thought him crazy and told him so. They hardly knew each other, she said. Yet Clyde persisted, and days later, he asked her to marry him again. Again she said no.

Clyde went to see Zena to tell her, over several cups of coffee, about the recent events in his life. He told Zena about the young woman he had met at Aunt Willie's, and how she had struck him as the picture of radiance and beauty.

"She has the most…the most…unusual and beautiful name," Clyde said. "I don't think I've ever heard one like it before."

"You don't say," said Zena. "What would her name be?"

He drew the name out and breathed it as he spoke. "Eve," he said. "Her name is Eve. Have you ever heard such a name in your life?"

"Yes, I have," said Zena. "That's the name of the first woman in the Bible."

Eve had been a popular young lady before coming to work for Clyde's Aunt Willie. Eve went out frequently, sometimes so much that she would tell her sister she was sick of men. She would shut herself away from them for a spell and refuse to go on another date, and then after a time, she would begin going out again and repeat the cycle. She had had proposals for marriage, and had turned down all but the last. The last of her suitors had been debonair and dashing and had showered her with gifts and devoted attention. As things go, however, things didn't continue well between Eve and her suitor. In time the relationship stumbled and began to fall apart, and through a series of circumstances, the suitor vanished, leaving Eve with only his ring, which she kept among her keepsakes in a jewelry box. On occasion she would take it out and wear it.

It happened that on a certain day in October, she was wearing the ring, sitting in the parlor of her parents' house, when there was a knock on the door. It was Clyde, who was paying a visit, unannounced. He had asked her hand in marriage on several occasions and had been refused each time; this time, he decided, he couldn't live without her, and had set his hat on making her his bride.

Eve did not know the reason for Clyde's visit. She was completely surprised to see him, unannounced as he was, and bold as ever. She stood before him, looking very much the same as the first time her saw her. She hesitated. Remembering she was wearing the engagement ring, she shifted her left hand behind her back. She bade Clyde come in. They sat in the parlor and talked. They exchanged some social niceties, he mentioning how unseasonably warm the weather was for October, and she nodding in agreement, still wondering why he had showed up to see her at her parents' house. When there was a lull in the conversation, Clyde said he had something to show her. As he spoke, he reached inside his coat pocket, withdrew a small box and opened it. Inside was an engagement ring. "Let me see your hand," he said. Eve reluctantly brought her hand from behind her back. Clyde took her hand in his. "What's this?" he said, seeing her ring. It looked as if another beau had beaten him to the punch.

"Oh," said Eve, flushing with color, "that's a ring from –"

Clyde didn't let her finish the sentence. "It won't do," he said. "This just won't do. Mine is prettier." He removed the ring from Eve's finger and replaced it with his own. In the same action, he asked her to marry him. Startled, surprising even herself with her response, Eve said yes.

"I know what I want," said Clyde later, "and I go after it." He would often tease Eve and others in attendance that he got married because he *had to* – and then quickly explain that he had to marry Eve because he couldn't live without her.

In part because Clyde couldn't wait to marry her, and in part because he thought it a nice tip of the hat to her most amazing, most beautiful name, they married on Christmas Eve, 1938. Everyone wished them well. Everyone except for Aunt Willie, who would hold it against Clyde for years following the wedding that he had "come and taken away her best help."

# Chapter 21: Cracking Diamonds

The year 1939 marked the end of some things and the beginnings of others. It was the end of Amelia Earhart, America's darling of aviation, now officially declared dead after her disappearance in the Pacific; it was the end of public guillotining in France, and the simultaneous ascendancy of philosophical polar opposites Mahatma Gandhi and Francisco Franco. It was the year of goldfish swallowing on college campuses, the New York World's Fair, the first sale of nylon stockings, and CBS Television. In 1939 two blockbuster movies, *The Wizard of Oz*, and *Gone with the Wind*, burst upon the American scene; while in Europe, Hitler's fulminations and invasion of Poland drew the world into a second great war.

Early in the year, Clyde got a job as a brakeman for Southern Pacific railroad. With irregular hours, being on call 24 hours a day, and an overseeing management that could be deaf and unforgiving, working for the railroad was unlike any job Clyde had taken on. The tools of his trade were simple: steel-toed work shoes, a lantern and the most accurate timepiece available. The pay, however, was quite good, and the work itself wasn't too difficult. It was just aggravating. Clyde would often say that the railroad could take a person who came into life happy-go-lucky and downright ruin his disposition after a few years.

Southern Pacific didn't tolerate mistakes, because even the smallest mistake could lead to the expensive disaster of train derailments and lost cargo and revenue. As a constant reminder of the company's attitude, Clyde carried in his pocket a Southern Pacific pencil characteristically devoid of an eraser – and the memory from his first day of work that there was no eraser for a good reason. Erasers, the foreman barked at him, are for people who make mistakes. "We don't make 'em, and you better not, you better get it right the first time, or you won't be working for long."

So to Clyde's small toolkit he added a circular slide rule for "mistake insurance," and the lucky gold nugget he had panned while in California. He had a jeweler attach a loop to it and carried it as a talisman, out of sight, in a pocket within a pocket, everywhere he went.

Yet, as much as the fear of failure had been impressed on him, he was drawn irresistibly to the Casey Jones aspect of railroading: the derailment, the train wreck, more impressive even than the destructive power of dynamite. Whenever he heard of a derailment, and if it wasn't too far out of his way to attend the scene, he would travel, camera in hand, and take numerous photos. He would walk around the wreckage, inspecting it from close and far, marveling all the while at the impact of cars thrown against each other into a crumpled, still smoking mass of steel.

Someone before him had been witness to such a wreck and had couched it in the language of the railroad engineer. Clyde carried it in his wallet for years. It was an accident report, told to the presiding judge by a boomer brakeman, in an attempt to explain how another train had happened to collide with his own. The brakeman reportedly said,

*"We just pulled the drag off the main stem onto the two streaks of rust but she hung over. The hoghead was down on the ground greasing the pig, and the tallowpot was up cracking diamonds. The con was in the doghouse flipping his tissues and the hind shack was cooling a red hub when he should have been trying to put 15 sticks between him and the drag. I was up ahead bending the rail when the streak of varnish and plate glass came around the bend. The eagle eye seen us and throwed her in the big hole and gave her two streams of seashore, but they had been pounding her on the back and they slid into us."*

*(Translation:*

*We had just pulled the local off of the main line onto a rarely used siding, but she had not cleared the main line. The engineer was down on the ground greasing the engine, the fireman was up in the tender breaking up coal. The conductor was in the caboose doing his paper work and the flagman was tending to a hot box when he should have been back at least 15 ties back on the main line with a flag. I was up ahead throwing a switch when here came this passenger train around the curve. The engineer saw us and put the emergency brake on and sanded the rail, but he was going very fast and they slid into us.)*

---

With a first child on the way, Clyde and Eve bought property in Sanderson, and he built a small, 2-bedroom house with his own hands. It was a white, pier-and-beam construction, clapboard house with a gabled roof and a storage attic. Rather than pay an electrician to wire the home, Clyde enrolled in a correspondence course, became a certified electrician, and wired the house himself.

He was proud of the house, standing there as it was in an almost vacant lot in the northeast area of Sanderson, the polished concrete steps to the front door guarded first by seedling juniper bushes, then by grape-motif concrete urns. He had staked his claim to the land and stamped it with a token of civilized development.

As he stood admiring his work, he was surprised that Eve's admiration wasn't as full and round as his own. She wished – oh, how she wished – it had a basement. A basement was something she had always desired in a home. This one Clyde had constructed was almost ideal. However, it didn't have a basement. Clyde promised his new bride he would consider the matter, but that it was a little late in the building process to add a basement, and even having one at all would be a considerable cost. He repeatedly told her he would think on the matter, not sure in his own mind how he would resolve it.

Beverly was born to the two admiring parents in November of 1939.

In December of 1941, when America entered the war against Japan and Germany, Clyde went to the local draft board and volunteered to join the Navy. It was a great disappointment to him when he was refused. Both his brother Johnny and brother-in-law Buster had joined the war effort soon after hostilities had commenced. Most of his friends he had known since childhood had signed up, and his best friend had joined the submarine service. Clyde went twice more to the draft board, now even more insistent and emphatic about enlisting. Each time he was refused.

"Why," he asked the board, emotion in his voice, "do you keep turning me down? I'd be the best damned soldier you ever had." When he was told that it was because of his job with SP that he couldn't join the service, that Uncle Sam considered him more valuable hauling freight than taking up arms, Clyde gave up volunteering. His job kept him out of the war. Some would have thought that a blessing, but Clyde didn't. He swallowed his disappointment and continued to run freight throughout the war.

Dorothy, Clyde and Eve's second child, was born on D-Day, June 6, 1944.

At the War's end, both Johnny and Buster returned home. However, neither Clyde's best friend, nor any of his crew, was ever heard from again. They simply disappeared without a trace. Clyde didn't mourn his friend's loss, because he never accepted the possibility of his being taken by the war. He held out hope that someday, somehow, he would return. "He was like me," Clyde said. "He could have gotten out of any situation. If there was any way in Hell for him to get out, he would have done it."

August 14, 1945 marked Victory over Japan, and the end of the War. Clyde Louis Jr., the third of Clyde and Eve's children, was born June 10$^{th}$ of the following year. Terry was born two years later, June 26, 1948.

Following Terry's birth, Clyde began hearing rumors of a government program to send cattle inspectors into Mexico in order to fight hoof-and-mouth disease. It would be dangerous work in the jungles of a developing country. Clyde's interest piqued, and he followed the rumor. It had awakened in him his wanderlust, his long-neglected need for fresh new adventure.

# Chapter 22: Mexico

Clyde liked a good yarn. Yarns, hunting and fishing stories, situational stories of close calls and near misses – sometimes indistinguishable from each other – served as entertainment in his days as a cowhand while he and the other ranch workers rested from the day's work and sat around the campfire. Clyde had his repertoire of yarns and liked to slip them in unannounced on the back of an otherwise mundane recounting of the day's events. He would begin with the phrase, "...kind of like this ol' boy that (did such and such") and thus launch the tale. One of his favorites dealt with a poor, simple ol' boy, flat busted, out on the prairie, walking along the railroad tracks, reduced to accepting whatever taunts fate could throw at him. Judging his familiarity with the story, listeners often wondered if the protagonist of the tale of diminishing choices was in effect Clyde himself.

*This old boy was walking along the railroad at night. There was no moon or stars to light his way, and he found the simplest and safest route he could take was the railroad tracks. So he walked along, putting one foot in front of another until he came to what looked like some sort of bridge. He had to make a decision. The question was, 'Should he cross it?' Too much trouble to go back, and besides, his luck was holding out pretty good so far. Probably wouldn't be any trains come along, so he took a chance and continued his path onto the bridge.*

*When he reached a point he judged to be about the middle of the span, he heard a train whistle. He stopped, not knowing what to do. He couldn't go back, because he wasn't sure which direction the train was coming from, and he couldn't go forward, because he didn't think he could get to the end of the bridge before the train overtook him. As the noise of the train grew louder, the old boy knew that the only choice he had was to climb down between some railroad ties and hold on until the train passed. Anyway, it was probably a short train, and he could crawl back up once it had gone over.*

*But it wasn't a short train. It was one of those long ones that haul over a hundred cars. So he hung there in and waited. He counted the cars as they rumbled overhead. The muscles in his arms and shoulders burned from holding his weight, but he couldn't let go, because the drop to the ground might kill him.*

*Finally the train passed. The old boy was so tired from holding on to the ties that he didn't have the strength to lift himself up. What should he do? He had no choice but to hang on until daylight and reassess his situation. His muscles ached so much it almost made him cry. Still he gripped the ties, holding on for dear life.*

*When it became light enough to see, he looked down to find his toes had been about six inches off the ground the whole time. Why, he could have let go at anytime during the whole ordeal and just walked away. Worse yet, if he had just wiggled his toes once, he would have felt the ground beneath him.*

*Made him so mad he just hung there the rest of the day.*

---

With the appointment with government USDA official approach-ing, and after that, his entry into Mexico, Clyde determined not to be like the ol' boy in the campfire tale. In the spring of 1949 he met with a government agent and to go over and sign the contract that would make him part of the Mexican-American commission for the eradication of aftosa fever. The requirements stipulated two things: that he have experience working with cattle and that he be fluent in Spanish. Meeting those requirements would net him what was considered a king's ransom at the time, approximately 165% of the average income in America in 1948 – plus, they threw in per diem for good measure.

Clyde quickly checked the first box, the one asking if he had experience working cattle, almost muttering 'silly question' as he did so. He was born and raised a cowboy; he was brought up on a ranch; and he had spent a good deal of his young life punching, roping and bronco busting.

The second box gave him pause. Spanish fluency. He was not fluent in Spanish by any means – but he *could* be. He was a quick study. He spoke a little Spanish – more than his dad whose command of the language consisted of saying, "Come you stay me go," with a hint of accent thrown in. Clyde felt he could do anything he needed to do, learn anything he needed to, in order to master a given situation. Feeling the agent's eyes bearing on him, he confidently checked the Spanish fluency box, saying to himself again that he *could* be fluent, and that was that. He signed at the bottom and shook the hand of the USDA official.

So two weeks later, Clyde, knowing only rudimentary Spanish, and having never lived in a jungle environment, and having never before flown on an airplane, was squeezed into a twin engine DC-3 and on his way to the state of Veracruz. It would be an adventure, he thought, and he was quite right. Some would have thought him reckless, both in his decision to join the venture and in his misrepresentation of facts.

Two great airline tragedies commanded the headlines in the region of Veracruz from 1948 to 1949. The first, on July 4$^{th}$ of 1948, involved a DC-3 carrying a team of Aftosa, or hoof-and-mouth disease, commissioners and $40,000 in American money from Mexico City to Minatitlán which crashed into Mexico's highest peak: Pico de Orizaba. There were reportedly no survivors, although a set of footprints was found leading away from the site. Searchers never found anyone. The cause of the crash was undetermined.[7]

On September 26th of 1949, a renowned Mexican movie actress, Blanca Estela Pavón, was killed in a Dakota airliner along with 16 others when their flight crew lost its bearings in the fog and crashed into Popocatepetl volcano. Srta Pavón was 23 years old. She was headed towards her hometown of Minatitlán.[8]

Clyde's flight was without incident, if not boring. He landed in Minatitlán and was taken by taxi to the residence of a family the Aftosa Commission had placed him with in advance. Clyde was to live with the family until he could establish a base or network of local workers whose job it would be to support him in the jungle.

The family chosen by the Commission warmly accepted Clyde from the beginning. Despite Clyde's temporary shortcomings in the language, the father of the family of ten ceded to Clyde the distinguished head of table. For their part, the host family served Clyde as an intensive crash course in the language and culture. In the end, they would enable Clyde to keep the internal vow he had made to the USDA official to become fluent.

In pursuit of his goal to master Spanish, Clyde thus abandoned every notion, every vestige of his own language. He interacted with members of the family on a daily basis. He shared in household duties and in the necessary repair and maintenance of the home. He partook of their food, listened to their stories at the dinner table, and told a few of his own. He grabbed what books he could lay his hands on, reading from cover to cover one in particular, a religious treatise explaining God's work on earth, titled *Que has hecho la religion por la humanidad?* He pored over daily newspaper accounts of life in and around Minatitlán. He practiced his Spanish in the marketplace and among the alligator farmers, and sellers of flowers and monkeys. His face tanned in the sun; he grew a pencil-thin mustache much like those sported by the denizens of Minatitlán; and at the end of two months, dressed in traditional loose-fitting white garb, standing among the fishermen on the quay of the Rio Coatzacoalcos, haggling, gesticulating like a music conductor, Clyde was indistinguishable from any other Mexican born and raised there.

---

[7] Source: AAP

[8] Source: AAP

# Chapter 23: Life in the Jungle

The Aztecs had called the little spot that lay within one of the coils of the Rio Coatzacoalcos “the place of the archers.” And though there were few actual archers who walked along the rolling, undulating streets of Minatitlán in 1949, the spirit of the archer – which could only be understood as a readiness to answer provocation with armed combat – was manifested from the confines of the city of bougainvillea and fan palms outward into the jungles.

Acting in the capacity of inspector for hoof-and-mouth disease, Clyde would spend an inordinate amount of time in the jungle. More often than not, he and his crew dealt with recalcitrant, irate ranchers, many of whom would have happily killed him.

The Mexican government, well aware of the fate of Clyde’s predecessors – the stoning of an inspector in Michoacan, and some 200 other inspectors ambushed in other parts – offered him the use of its military, by which Clyde could more easily coerce the local ranchers into turning over their cattle to him.

But Clyde refused the offer out of hand. He didn’t think use of the military would aid his mission one iota. Besides, it looked cowardly. He would deal with the ranchers in his own way. He believed he could persuade them through reason, from the point of view of a fellow *vaquero,* someone who had worked on ranches much of his life, and understood their mentality and their way of life. And in the end, one by one, he would win them over.

Many times, Clyde and his men had to cut through overgrown trails to get to his assignments. On his first meeting with the ranchers, Clyde would sit down with them, often over cordial drinks of tequila and *pulque,* and discuss the situation they were in, that their bad cattle had to be culled and the healthy ones inoculated against the disease called *aftosa*. He noted that the job wasn’t easy, and that no two cases were the same.

On one of his forays into the jungle, a log that apparently fallen across the trail prevented him and his crew from traveling further. A closer look however, revealed that the obstruction was not a log, but an immense python. When asked what the team should do, Clyde said, “We’ll wait.” “Let the python cross the road in his own good time; I’m not of a mind to tangle with him this morning.” And they waited. They sat on the fenders of the truck, sharpened their machetes, smoked cigarettes, and swatted mosquitoes. After about an hour, the python crawled off into the underbrush, and Clyde and his crew continued on their way, heading deeper into the jungle.

As for their work clothes, they adopted a uniform that was loose fitting and bleach white: a Mexican wedding shirt, cotton duck trousers and wide-brimmed hats. And as they traveled in search of the large cattle ranches, they would come across primitive communities of indigenous people wearing either a decorative patch of oilskin in strategic areas or nothing at all, working, talking, going about the business of their daily lives, dropping everything to gaze in wonder at the overdressed outsiders brandishing machetes.

"They didn't hide many secrets," Clyde would later say.

The villagers were useful in setting Clyde and his crew right in their trail, if they had lost it, or pointing them towards clean water sources. They were simple and carefree, and happy in their lives, Clyde noted. They presented no problem for him. That would come with the more civilized people. It was on the ranches where he was tested.

Even after getting to know the ranchers and working alongside them, Clyde would be presented with tests of cultural machismo: ardent questions of who among them could drink the most, the locals or the outsider; or who showed more courage and prowess in a duel. And Clyde knew that failure to make a good or superior showing could affect the success of his campaign.

Once, after a hard day of rounding up and inoculating cattle, the owner brought out several bottles of tequila along with shot glasses. "Do you think you can drink with us?" he asked Clyde. "Which of us will remain standing?"

It was not the kind of contest Clyde relished, but he accepted and entered into it. The drinking went on late into the night, the host watching Clyde closely, waiting for him to falter. But Clyde put on a brave front and matched the men drink for drink. They talked, they laughed, and they played the accordion in front of onlookers. As Clyde scanned the room with bleary eyes, he noticed fewer participants. A couple of them lay on the floor, asleep. He steeled himself with each new drink. Every time he looked around, he noticed more of them passed out.

At last it was just himself and the ranch owner, sitting across the table from each other. Clyde thought since they were the only ones left, they should call it a draw and congratulate each other. With difficulty he tried to form the words. Nothing was said. Instead, he reached his hand out to shake the owner's hand. Before a very surprised Clyde, the man closed his eyes and slumped to the floor.

Clyde arose and walked as soberly as he could out of the room. He turned to tip his sombrero to the onlookers and bid them good night, thinking he had pronounced "*buenas noches*" fairly well, and headed towards his quarters. Hardly did he get to the bunkhouse and pass through the door, when he tumbled into his bed and into the darkness of unconsciousness.

But he had won. More than that, he had left the locals with the impression that he was invincible.

In the months that followed, Clyde lived a life very similar to that of other American inspectors in Veracruz. Like them, he lived off the land for weeks or months, in primitive country, going from one estate to the next, dealing with ranchers who smiled to his face, but seemed strangely bent on killing him.

His crew diminished weekly, through either disease or homesickness. Towards the end of his first campaign in the jungle, Clyde found himself a leader of not much, and with dwindling supplies. On a certain ranch, one on which he had befriended the proprietor and was attempting to take a break in the shady back area of the estate, just as he held a cup of coffee to his mouth and took a sip, a worker came running up to him.

"*Patron!*" he said, "There is a man in the corral with a machete and he says he wants to fight with you. He also told me he will kill you."

Clyde looked out into the cow pen and saw the man in the distance, dressed in white baggy clothes, swinging his machete in wide arcs, cursing loudly, and appearing quite drunk. "Bring me the gringo!" Clyde heard him say.

The messenger waited for Clyde to give an answer. "Go back and tell him I will be there directly," Clyde said, "right after I finish my cup of coffee."

Later, the messenger returned again to Clyde's table.

"He says he has had enough of your waiting. He wants you to come down this minute to fight him," he said.

"Ask him to wait a little longer," Clyde said, draining the last of his coffee. "I'll be there." The messenger did so. Clyde arose to walk to his truck and pick out a machete. With it in hand, he walked down to the corral. But when he reached it, he looked around and saw no one but the messenger, leaning against a rail.

"Where 's the man?" Clyde asked.

"Over there," he said. "He passed out. He's sleeping now."

"I can't fight a sleeping man," said Clyde, "so I guess it's no contest." He slipped his machete into the scabbard and walked away.

On one of his campaigns into the jungle, Clyde killed a jaguar, and the locals skinned it and tanned the hide for him. On another campaign, he captured as personal pets two spider monkeys, which he named Cuca and Chico.

He had finished a good year and was looking forward to getting back to Minatitlán and enjoying the creature comforts of home in a modern bed, good food and clean water – but towards the end of his tour, he found himself in a difficult situation. All his men had either fallen sick or had deserted. He had to carry medical supplies to the next village east, but the rains had washed out the trails. Both Clyde and the villagers knew that the only means left open to him was by canoe down river, and that since time was of the essence, he had to travel at night.

"Don't worry," they assured him. "You won't travel the river alone; we'll send a *brujo* with you. He says he wants a ride to the next village anyway."

That night, the two of them set out, Clyde and the local witch doctor, and floated in the wide part of the river under a pitch-black moonless sky. The *brujo* didn't say much. He wore feathers and beads and his features were drawn. While Clyde paddled, the *brujo sa*t in the canoe, sometimes folding his arms, sometimes dragging his fingers in the water.

The farther they went down river, the higher the trees grew, and the darker their trip became. Clyde soon lost sight of the banks on either side of him, and not knowing where he was, he ran aground. Then he got out, dislodged the canoe, and recommenced his journey only to drift into a dead mango grove. He thought he heard the witch doctor chuckle. Cautiously, Clyde recommenced, trying to stay in the center of the river, the deepest part, as best he was able. But he was never sure where the center was.

Try as he might, he couldn't help but strike another sand bar a few minutes later. Again, he pushed the canoe away, swearing under his breath.

The *brujo,* silent until now, and probably feeling compassion, told Clyde that he should "look for the light."

"What light?" said Clyde.

"The silver ribbon of light that runs along down there, like a serpent."

Clyde looked hard, but saw nothing on the black water. "There's no light," he said.

"Look again," said the *brujo.* "Don't look at the water; look *through* the water. The light is down there. It runs only in the deepest part of the river.

Do you see it?"

Clyde did as the old man said, and tried to look through the water. He looked carefully; he squinted, turning his head from side to side. And then he thought he saw it – a faint, intermittent, glimmer of light. "Yes, I do see it!" Clyde said.

"Where does that light come from?" he asked, in full wonder.

"I don't know," said the *brujo,* "Just follow it."

Clyde continued to paddle downstream, making use of the old man's magic, staying above the ghost-like light in order to navigate the river. He was elated at the discovery; as if a secret of the ancients had been revealed to him, and he savored it with every touch of the paddle to the dark water.

The two of them arrived in the neighboring community just before dawn. After Clyde guided the dugout ashore, he and the old man parted ways.

Per Clyde and Eve's original plans, she and the four children came to stay with him in Mexico after his first year. They stayed a short while in Minatitlán, living in a modest home buried among tropical trees and vegetation only a stone's throw from the alligator farm, as Beverly remembered. Then Clyde moved them all to Mexico City, quite distant from where Clyde's work was. He set Eve up in luxurious elements: a large and comfortable house with thick walls and tiled floors – colorful and bright in the Mexican style of the homes – and hired a maid to help out with managing the household.

For almost a year, Eve enjoyed the pampered life of a duchess, albeit one who witnessed while on her way to market, an occasional dead body lying in the gutter. Then, when Clyde's contract was up, they all returned to the United States, along with the spider monkeys, Cuca and Chico.

# Chapter 24: Pursuit of Happiness

The green and golden snake that was the Rio Grande glittered, and then slipped beneath the wings of the Douglas DC-3. Clyde considered it. At other less certain times, the river might almost have proved his better, but not now. For him, and at this time in his life (for he was only 40) anything was possible – or so it seemed. He was flying at 20,000 feet – higher than Pico de Orizaba. Soon he would be back at his own front door, returning victorious from two years in another country, emboldened and wealthier. His heart climbed in his chest. He was caught up in the extended euphoria of not just winning, but winning big – convinced beyond doubt he could do anything at all if he set his mind to it.

The last of the Whistler children, Jack, was born January 11, 1951. Clyde resumed his work for Southern Pacific, making railroad runs between Sanderson and Valentine, Texas. He had time and inclination to build. He acquired libraries on construction, welding, electricity, and wiring, and he learned them. He finished the basement Eve had so desired before the Mexico adventure. He built, it seemed, whatever occurred to him: a corrugated tin home for Cuca and Chico -- one big enough for them to play and screech to their hearts' contents -- a grape arbor, a set of monkey bars at the back of the lot for the kids, a workshop and shed. Through his library, he learned about radios and televisions and began first tinkering with, and then repairing them. Soon after, he hand-lettered his new trade on a 1954 Chevrolet truck. In a wide curving arch it read, C. L. WHISTLER ELECTRIC. The following year, he turned his radio shack into a grocery, and was proud of the sign he hand-lettered and mounted above the entrance: COMMUNITY CASH GROCERY. "Note that little word in the middle," he would tell people. "Cash. That means no credit. Cash on the barrel head." Striking one large tanned hand palm up into the other, he would laugh.

In those same years he pursued hobbies and interests, from photography, to cabinet making, word turning, and leatherwork, to participating as a catcher on the newly created Sanderson softball team. And he fished and hunted, fishing in the Rio Grande and all the local tributaries in between; hunting mostly deer both in and out of season, with or without a permit, cashing in on a cherished phrase he was fond of quoting from the Constitution: that he was entitled to life, liberty and pursuit of happiness.

His favorite person to go fishing with was not an able-bodied person like himself, but rather, a paraplegic package store owner named Mac. In this case, "package" was a euphemism for "liquor," but he sold other items as well, such as cigars and bottle openers, and the gaping skeletal jaws of a shark in the front window usually invited talk about his favorite pastime in healthier days: deep sea fishing. Camping out and fishing with Mac meant a great deal of extra work for Clyde, but he did so cheerfully. He would have to lift Mac in and out of the pickup, and in and out of the boat, and do everything for Mac except string his line and bait his hook. But as he told those who would question his taking a crippled man fishing, Clyde would say, "Mac enjoys it. I would rather go fishing with him than anyone else."

Anecdotes of his exploits grew. Phillip Eggleston, a coworker, spoke admiringly of Clyde as an interesting character who carried a circular slide rule (whoever heard of such a thing?) in a shirt pocket and talked about "triangulating" the positions of javelinas during a hunt.

Another coworker with whom he shared a pace in Valentine, complained (perhaps out of jealousy) that on too many occasions, Clyde would "get off the train, and go shoot deer."

His daughter Dotty once asked him what he did on the railroad, and Clyde replied, "I get blamed for things that happen while I'm not there," and he could easily have been referring to a derailment he was held responsible for in 1956. An investigation was called, and then a hearing. Clyde's job hung in the balance. Acting as his own counsel before what he privately referred to as a "kangaroo court," he out argued the Company attorney and was exonerated.

In the same year, he moved the family to Aransas Pass, Texas where he worked for John Pollard on a shrimp boat called *The Chief.* Clyde quickly learned the ropes of the shrimp trade and moved up the ladder. In very little time at all, he became captain of his own boat, *The Skipjack.* Named after a species of tuna, *The Skipjack* was not a very handsome boat -- white with green and red trim, extremely long and narrow -- and the other shrimpers had fun pointing out the oddity of the sight of the man in the weathered Stetson hat astride it, acting a bit differently from the average shrimper, throwing ropes and nets not like any of them at all, but like the cowboy he was, and they took pleasure in "hoorahing" Clyde when his boat passed theirs, hollering out, "Cowboy on a skipjack! Cowboy on a skipjack!" In whatever way the jibe was intended, whether derisively, or in good jest, Clyde accepted the distinction with pride, and quite enjoyed being singled out in that way by his fellows.

Louis Whistler once made it a personal goal to follow Clyde around and learn everything his Dad knew, all of which brought a tremendous grin to Clyde's face. At one point in his quest, Louis asked his father -- considering everything he had done in his life -- how he would like to be remembered. Clyde replied, "as a hunter, a fisherman, and as an outdoor person." He was very proud of his outdoor skills.

Along that line, Louis provides still further anecdotes and insights into Clyde's personality:

> Clyde Whistler was an outdoorsman - a hunter and a fisherman. Clyde grew up a cowboy, and he loved the outdoors. He was also somewhat of an egoist - he liked outdoor challenges, he liked solving problems, and he liked besting others at the outdoors crafts.
>
> Clyde came through the depression years with a character forged by doing what you had to do to make ends meet. There were no jobs when the depression hit, and many men where Clyde grew up began going on long trips to the Rio Grande River to catch fish for barter to acquire other needed services for their families.
>
> Among others, Clyde made ends meet by hauling supplies to the fishermen in his Model T coup. However, unlike the other supply couriers who were all tired of the frequent delays caused by flat tires, Clyde decided to do something about it. He saved a little money and purchased four solid rubber tires from Wards. He then ran a booming business as the courier with the fastest and most reliable service. He could go anywhere in that Model T and never had a flat. No one could tell that he was running on solid tires.
>
> Clyde's favorite destination was a place called Bone Water located 18 miles south of Sanderson. Bone Water was an excellent fishing spot but very difficult to reach because of the rugged terrain. Clyde was the only delivery person for that choice spot. Clyde did quiet well in those years.

> In the early1930s drought ravaged a large portion of the United States. Cattle and sheep ranchers had substantial herds of animals that were starving for lack of grazing and water. The ranchers could not afford to feed them, and many ranchers were on the verge of bankruptcy.
>
> In January of 1935, the federal government formed the Drought Relief Service (DRS) to coordinate relief activities. The DRS bought cattle and sheep for $14 to $20 a head in counties that are designated emergency areas. Those unfit for human consumption – more than 50 percent at the beginning of the program – were destroyed. The remaining sheep and cattle were given to the Federal Surplus Relief Corporation to be used in food distribution to families nationwide. Although it was

difficult for ranchers to give up their herds, the sheep and cattle slaughter program helped many of them avoid bankruptcy.

Clyde hired on as a cowboy to the DRS active in the counties surrounding Terrell County. On ranch after ranch, they herded sheep into pens and culled the starving sheep into singular large groups. The cowboys positioned themselves around these pens armed with lever action rifles. On cue, they slaughtered thousands of starving sheep that were then bulldozed into large pits, burned, and buried.

For their services, the cowboys were paid a decent wage of real money. It was not a proud time in Clyde's life, but he did what he had to do to make a living in hard times.

Both before and after Clyde spent two years in Mexico, he worked as a conductor on the Southern Pacific railroad with a central depot in Sanderson, Texas. Clyde rode regularly roundtrip on trains traveling the several hundred miles between Sanderson and the crew change point in Valentine.

Clyde's family had grown to five kids, and Clyde did not make a lot of money on the railroad. He felt he had to be versatile. However, he was too proud to take handouts.

Black tailed deer were plentiful in counties surrounding Terrell County. The cascading and rough semi-desert foothills that extended from Del Rio and Brackettville in the south, Ozona in the north, and Alpine and Marfa at the base of the Chisos mountains in the west were the ideal environment for deer. The deer were prolific all during Clyde's life.

Clyde hunted his limit during hunting season, but that did not take care of his family needs the remainder of the year. Clyde rationalized that the deer were plentiful, he had a need, and taking deer out of season did not hurt anybody. His brothers, sisters, and family felt the same. Besides, he was good at it.

During regular hunting seasons, Clyde sometimes walked for miles over the roughest terrain to find the deer. He often arose in the middle of the night to walk five to ten miles in pitch dark to get to an ideal hunting place before the deer got up from their bedding place. He was really good at walking long distance over rough passages, and he had an uncanny ability to do this in the dark. He scoffed at those that waited in blinds for deer to come to feeders. He said that was not "hunting" -- that was "hiding."

During the off season, Clyde frequently made nightly head-lighting trips on surrounding highways to harvest deer along the roadsides. He never took what his family did not need, and he never wasted any of his collections. He kept his freezer box full and his family well fed.

However, he operated a running gambit with the local game warden. On one occasion he was trapped on a backcountry ranch road by the warden in the late evening. Clyde escaped by driving much faster than the warden could across the roughest terrain directly into the setting sun. He escaped but returned home with a bullet hole in the rear fender of his Ford pickup. He repaired the damage himself.

On another out-of-season hunting occasion one late evening, Clyde became aware that the game warden was tailing him. Clyde parked his truck off the roadside, took his gun, climbed over a fence, and disappeared into the wilderness darkness. The warden parked his car behind some bushes nearby and waited for Clyde's return where he could nab him with his ill-gotten booty.

Instead, Clyde crossed ten miles of rough backcountry, bagged his deer, formed its legs into back-straps, and packed the deer out to another highway where he concealed it nearby. He hiked to a gas station and called a friend who picked him up and took him and his harvest home.

After butchering the deer and storing the meat in the freezer, Clyde changed clothes and hitchhiked back to his truck where the game warden waited. Clyde thanked his ride, got in his truck and drove home past the now "fuming" game warden.

On yet another midnight hunting occasion, Clyde was driving and had his cousin John Lewis with him to help. They had not been successful in finding a reasonable prey until the passed a ranch house near Pumpville located several miles to the west of Sanderson. Beside the road near the ranch house, an ideal sized buck was grazing in the dark. Clyde turned the pickup around toward Sanderson and stopped across from the deer.

Clyde told John Lewis to get that .22 rifle from behind the seat to shoot the deer. He did not want to awaken anyone in the ranch house. However, in the darkness inside the vehicle, John Lewis retrieved a much larger .270 rifle. The sound of the high-powered gun reverberated inside the truck and across to the ranch house. The deer dropped in its tracks.

To Clyde and John's astonishment, lights came on in the ranch house, and the game warden dashed out in his pajamas. He had been spending the night there.

Clyde jammed the gas pedal to the floor and sped off at speeds of up to 100 miles per hour with the flashing lights of the game warden trailing about a mile behind. Clyde zoomed over the top of a high hill, cut his lights, slammed on the breaks, and spun the pickup around. He put on his lights and floored the truck going the other direction. They passed the game warden at the top of the hill and watched in the rear view mirrors as he drove out of sight.

Clyde and John Lewis retrieved their booty, placed it in the back under a tarp, and headed back to Sanderson. On the way, they passed the game warden who had pulled over another car. A family stood beside the road as the game warden in his pajamas searched the car tossing its contents onto the roadside.

The next day, John Lewis reported that he saw the game warden in the Sanderson local coffee shop. John Lewis bought him a cup of coffee and asked him if he had caught any poachers recently. The warden said that he had caught some tourists just that night. They must have thrown the gun out the window, but he emptied their car beside the road. On top of losing the gun, they had a big cleanup job to do. In addition, he said, the deer got away. He doubted they would try poaching again.

John Lewis and the game warden had a laugh about it and parted ways.

Clyde had lots of guns. He had ten to fifteen rifles that ranged from .22s, a .25-35, a .30-40 lever action Krag, several .30-06s, a .270, and several pistols. Clyde loaded his own ammunition. One of the guns was a Mossberg show .22 that he acquired after he took Cuca and Chico (the spider monkeys he got from Mexico) to the San Antonio zoo.

Clyde was raised to be very careful with guns, and he taught his children the same. However, one time he was retrieving a gun by the barrel from behind the seat of his truck, the trigger caught on a loose seat wire, and the gun discharged, striking Clyde in the fleshy part of his forearm. The wound healed, but Clyde carried that scar for the rest of his life as a reminder to always be careful with guns and to always treat them as loaded and dangerous.

Clyde always carried a .45 pistol in his handbag when he worked on the railroad. He had heard of the famous train robbery just east of Sanderson by members of the Hole-in-Wall gang that had occurred quiet a few years previously. Clyde said that he would never allow himself to be captured like that without a weapon for protection.

On one outbound passage toward Valentine, Clyde was riding in the engine of a long train pulling over a hundred cars up a steep grade heading west, and the train was moving at a crawl. Clyde saw a nice size deer standing idly beside the track as the train approached. He retrieved the pistol from his handbag, stood on the train side rail, and shot the deer in its tracks as the train passed.

Clyde jumped from the train, cleaned the deer, made its legs into back straps, hoisted the deer onto his back, and jumped on the caboose as it passed. He dumped the deer beside the track shortly before they got to Valentine, checked out with his crew, retrieved the carcass, and hung it in the meat locker of a local restaurant.

He shared some of the meat with his friends in Valentine. However, little by little, he transferred the remainder back to his family in Sanderson in frozen packages carried in his work travel bag.

Each Thanksgiving during the early 1960's there was a turkey shoot contest held in Sanderson. Of course they really did not shoot turkeys. It was merely a shooting contest where the contestants paid money to shoot at targets. The idea was the 10 to 15 best scores got to take home free, live turkeys for their Thanksgiving meals. The net proceeds went to a local benefit.

Needless to say, that was the kind of thing that challenged Clyde's ego. Every year that he partici-pated, he brought home at least one turkey and usually several. Clyde was an excellent marksman.

One hunting season Clyde was hunting along with his cousin on the familiar Chisos Mountain haunts of his Uncle Terry Shely's 100-section ranch. They had been hunting all day without bagging a deer and stood at a mountain precipice overlooking a distant plain. Clyde scanned the scene below with high-powered binoculars and spotted a large, grazing buck more than 400 yards away. There was no way to sneak up to get closer to deer without alerting its attention.

Clyde was carrying an old military, lever action .30-40 Krag equipped with long distance, open windage sights. He decided that he was going to try and shoot that deer from where he was situated. He made a guess as to the distance, set his sight, propped the gun on a convenient boulder, took aim and fired.

After the blast and severe kick he trained his binoculars on the deer and watched. Several seconds later he saw a puff of dust short of but near the deer. The deer leapt and began running full speed directly away from Clyde.

He adjusted his wind sight, gave a little higher elevation and fired a second time. A few seconds later he saw another puff of dust behind the running deer but closer. Clyde fired two more shots, each time setting his sight a little higher and thus additionally elevating the gun barrel -- he was walking the shots into the deer. On the last shot, he set the sight on the maximum of 600 yards and raised the gun barrel a little higher. After that fourth shot, he observed a puff of hair from between the deer's shoulder blades and the deer went down.

Clyde and his cousin walked the distance to the deer and they estimated that the final shot was approximately 700 yards.

Clyde purchased an International Harvester Scout with four-wheel drive. He owned a mule.

One hunting season Clyde organized a hunting trip to Colorado with his friends, one of many that would later follow. He loaded up the Scout with supplies, put his mule in a small horse trailer, and made the trip to Colorado. After two weeks he returned to Sanderson with his mule and a full complement of bagged deer.

He began telling the story of an "old boy" in Colorado who brought three mules - one for riding and two for packing supplies. He said that one night this old boy decided to do some head lighting for wild game. The old boy walked from his encampment down and around the peak of the hill shining his flashlight and looking for the reflection in the eyes of wild animals.

After a while the old boy spotted two eyes shining in the light. He fired one shot and dropped the animal. Then, he saw another set of eyes, and he fired again and downed that animal. Then, he saw another set of eyes and fired away and bagged that animal as well.

The old boy approached his prey and discovered that he had shot and killed his own mules.

Clyde said that the moral of this story is two-fold - be sure of what you are shooting at and don't be greedy.

During the shrimping season in 1958, Clyde took a three-month leave of absence from the railroad so that he could work for a hunting buddy of his who owned a shrimp boat. Shrimping had been good, and Clyde stood to make a substantial amount more than his railroad paycheck.

Clyde took his family, a dog and two cats and moved them into a rental house in Aransas Pass, Texas. His children joined the local schools, and he started the hard work of a deck hand on a shrimping boat.

On September 6, 1958 Hurricane Ella made landfall in southern Texas near Corpus Christi with winds of 45 mph. Although most of the shrimpers made it to safe harbor, Clyde's shrimp boat was caught in the open ocean where they decided to ride out the storm.

They pointed the boat into the waves and had to gun the engine to prevent it falling off one way or the other since the waves were so high. When they reached the peak, they had to cut the throttle to prevent over-revving the engine when the stern came out of the water.

The captain mused that he wished it were daylight so that he could see what they were doing. Later, when daylight came, he quipped that he wished it was dark so that he would not have to see how big the waves were. Clyde spent the daylight hours roped to battens on the bow and taking pot shots with a .22 at flying fish as they leaped from the waves.

After many hours of battling the storm, the boat had taken on considerable water and they were in peril. The captain decided to beach the boat on Padre Island and escape with whatever they could. The captain radioed an SOS to the Coast Guard and they headed for the beach.

The boat bumped once, lurched, turned sideways and slammed into the shore. The crew scrambled onto the beach and huddled in the safety of the dunes as they watched the tremendous waves batter the boat to driftwood.

When the storm cleared, Clyde made a fire on the beach. Before the day was out, a Coast Guard helicopter picked them up and returned then to civilization.

Just before the storm, three small communities, including Aransas pass where Clyde's family was living, had been evacuated. As Ella made landfall, tides were reported at 3 ft above mean sea level and rainfall peaked at 13 in. There were many shrimp boats damaged or destroyed in the storm, but there was only one person killed offshore by Hurricane Ella in 1958.

Clyde did not make much money that year, but he returned the next year to work on a larger shrimp boat and did quiet well.

In 1962 Clyde decided to take his family on a fishing trip. He picked a location on the West Coast of Mexico that he had learned about when he was an agent doctoring cattle for Aftosa hoof-and-mouth disease. They were to be joined by the family of Clyde's brother-in-law.

Clyde owned a 16-foot aluminum boat carried on a trailer that he had welded. He bought an old 3/4-ton Metro delivery van and got to work making modifications. He cleared the inside of the cabin except of the front two bucket seats and installed a large ice chest for groceries on the way down and fish on the way back. Clyde also modified the boat trailer to carry nine 20-gallon fuel drums for his boat motor and two high-pressure air cylinders for the family's Scuba tanks.

The families set out on their trip with children finding seating as they could on top of camping gear and supplies stacked in the back of the Metro. They drove to El Paso, through New Mexico, and on to Arizona. They turned south at Tucson and crossed into Mexico at Nogales, Arizona. They drove through the Sonora desert to Hermosillo and then to Guaymas on the Pacific waters of the Gulf of California where they loaded the now empty ice chest with dry ice.

The families continued on to their fishing site traveling down back roads, over dry creeks and along gullies and getting stuck many times. Clyde used his jungle experience with winches, tree branch levers, and shovels to extract them each time. They finally reached their destination of a small Mexican fishing camp at a beautiful, well-protected cove.

The families pitched their camps with army cots for sleeping on the beach. Clyde put his boat in the water and began making daily fishing trips to the nearby rock islands jutting out of the sea that were named

Piedras Negras and Piedras Blancas (black rock and white rock). The kids often times went with him, but usually spent their time exploring the adjacent coves and Scuba diving in the beautiful warm blue water. The Mexican fishermen taught the kids how to eat raw scallops.

At the trip's end they headed back, extracted several times from extreme incidents by Clyde's jungle skills. The family returned home to Sanderson with over 200 lbs. of frozen fish along with meat from a large *tortuga* (sea turtle), which was a present from the Mexican fishermen.

The many things Clyde built and accomplished in the 1950s, his experiences, and the stories that were told about him, gave witness to a man whose potential had been unleashed, and for whom the world was his private oyster. He often told people he could do anything he set his mind to do. But in 1956 he caught wind of the Padre Island Walkathon. He was 44. Was he too old? Could he still compete? Could he beat the local hero? It would become his obsession for the three years.

While working in the Gulf Coast area, Clyde got wind of the Padre Island Walkathon, which was a three-day, 40-mile walking race covering the length of the island and back. The prizes were generous and the competition fierce. An enigmatic athlete named Charles Reilly won First Place in the contest year after year. Clyde saw the Walkathon as a challenge; he accepted it. He set his cap on toppling Reilly from his perch.

After returning from the Gulf Coast, he sent in his entry fee for the next Walkathon and began his training for the event. He ceased his consumption of junk food and alcohol, and he practiced three days a week, three hours per session, on an isolated dirt airstrip at the edge of town, traveling from one end of the strip to the other, adopting the peculiar squatting-style walk that Reilly employed, walking in this way faster than most people his age could run.

# Chapter 23: Padre Island Walkathons

In 1953, in an ambitious effort to bring attention to the "Fisherman's Paradise" which was Padre Island, the City Fathers instituted the athletic contest of the Walkathon. It was a race over 110 miles, from tip to tip of the Island and back, and the rule was simple: it had to be walked – no running allowed. Walking was defined as "always keeping one foot on the ground." It was open to all comers, young and old, male and female, and the entrance fee was $10.00. James Outlaw was the winner in 1954; he went on to win trophies in 100 other races, but always looked back on the Padre Island Walkathon as "the toughest race in the world," and the winning of it as the thing he was most proud of in his life.

Clyde tried out in 1955, mainly to test the waters and to get a feel for the competition. Early in the race, he ran (walked, rather) through a puddle of water; his shoes shrank, he got blisters, and had to drop out. Dotty Whistler remembered going with him to shop for a new pair of running shoes at Kerr's in Sanderson. "He told me that he used to wear 10 1/2, but 11's felt so good he bought 12's!"

But in the 1955 race, Clyde had got his first look at Riley, the person he would have to beat to win the race. Charley Riley was a 27-year-old track coach from Victoria, Texas, who did everything differently from the rest of the competition – from walking to eating to sleeping. He had his own style of walking – a rapid, unnatural-appearing, almost comic half-squat – looking more like a Groucho Marx impersonator than a competitive walker. But that style allowed him to move at a quick pace and yet stay within the rules, always having one foot on the ground. He refused most of the refreshments that were offered during the competition, limiting himself to oranges, salt tablets and water. At night he slept with his feet elevated.

Of all Riley's quirks, Clyde chose to adopt only the walking style. Over the following years, he would praise it as superior to any other, and he practiced it religiously. In 1956, Clyde trained as often as he was able on whatever flat land was available to him in Sanderson. The highlight of his training, however, was only obliquely associated with his practicing the half-crouch. It involved an encounter that took place out in the country among the prickly pear and creosote. Clyde, after much walking, searched for a place to relieve himself. He thought he had found just the correct spot when he thought he heard the familiar clicking sound of a rattlesnake. The clicking turned into a loud rattle and Clyde finally saw the large snake coiled directly in front of him, ready to strike. Keeping his eye on the snake, he reached behind him, feeling for a rock, when he heard another rattler. He gathered his composure, and was moving ever so carefully away from the two snakes when he awakened a third snake. “How many snakes *are* there?” he wondered aloud. He looked around, widening his gaze. There were four, five, six snakes. He was surrounded! All told, he counted a dozen. Outnumbered as he was, there was nothing to do but retreat; he slowly threaded his way out of the mess he had walked into, left the snakes in peace, and took his business elsewhere.

In 1956, Clyde came in seventh place in the race. It had been grueling. He was dog-tired, sunburnt and blistered. He had done his best. He was almost 45. The Corpus Christi Times reported the event as follows:

> (*Corpus Christi Times*, June 4, 1956)
> **RILEY WINS WALKATHON, SETS RECORD**
>
> Charley Riley, 28-year-old track coach from Bloomington, was richer by $700, a used car, 100 gallons of gasoline, a snack bar and two chicken dinners today after setting a new record yesterday in the fourth annual Padre Island Walkathon.
>
> Riley walked the 110-mile race up Padre Island sand in a total time of 20 hours, 3 minutes, which is 56 minutes faster than the record time he set last year to win the race. He averaged nearly 6 miles an hour on the final day of the three-day race.

The article went on to name C. L. Whistler as one of the winners, with a time of 26 hours, 41 minutes.

No race took place in 1957. In an interview, just before the 1958 race, Riley was garrulous, talking of training for 800 miles to get ready for the event, being trim, tan and hard because of long hours of training. “I’d like to set a steady pace,” he said, “but I’m not going to let anybody get far ahead of me. If someone wants to set a fast pace in the first 2 miles, I’m going to keep up with him.” He finished by saying he expected to win.

As much in response to Riley’s article as to boost his self-confidence, Clyde placed a short article of his own in the Sanderson Times. In a small, off-chance way, he hoped Riley would see it:

> My name is Clyde Whistler. I can walk farther and faster and shoot more deer in these hills than any other man in Terrell County. I am the best runner and the best hunter around. This summer I will compete in the Padre Island Walkathon and win.

To prepare for the race, Clyde took on a strict, lean diet. He consumed no alcohol, soft drinks, chocolates or candies. He traveled to a little-used dirt airport just east of the Deaton ranch and practiced Riley's crouch-style walk three hours a day. At the time of the race in May, Clyde too was "trim, tan and hard." Riley had lost 10 lbs to weigh 140; Clyde had lost 35 lbs to weigh 165. He felt like a boxer in peak condition. Once again, he felt as if he could do anything. He had thrown himself into this race with great determination. Winning it – toppling Riley – was his dream.

After the race, the following article appeared in a local paper:

**CLYDE WHISTLER PLACES FOURTH IN WALKATHON**
*(Dated June 6, 1958)*

Clyde Whistler of Sanderson was fourth place winner in the 40-mile Padre Island Walkathon last Sunday. Whistler, who is 48, was the oldest contestant and finished in seven hours and 20 minutes. He has competed in the Walkathon for several consecutive times and improves his speed each year. He walked from 20 to 30 miles daily here to get in condition for the Walkathon.

The previous walkathons were 110 miles long and lasted for three days.

Charley Riley, former Bloomington track coach and now an insurance agent in Victoria, finished the walkathon in five hours, eight minutes and 22 seconds, averaging 7.8 miles per hour in winning his third Walkathon.

"Pretty damned good for a 48-year-old man," Clyde said. But in fact, his last-ditch gambit had failed. After 1958, there would be no more Walkathons. The City Fathers wouldn't continue promoting the "Fisherman's Paradise" in that particular way, and Clyde felt he didn't have it in him if they had. After his last great race, he turned his mind towards other less strenuous pursuits, principal among them the practice of flying small aircraft.

# Chapter 26: Into an Open Field

With his near glory as a distance walker becoming now just another memory of bygone days and things that could have been, and with the great decade of the 50s drawing to a close, Clyde found himself wistful, looking back over his life. He was often heard to say, "I was born with the automobile, and I have lived to see a man orbit the earth." And yet he scoffed at what he considered the foolhardiness of the government and its agencies, especially concerning their experiments and the wasting of taxpayers' money. When Clyde heard the Army had developed a "gun" powerful enough to fire bullets at the moon, his interest was piqued, and he would read the newspapers everyday to see what the Army would do. It happened without much fanfare. There on page three of the San Angelo Times was a story almost as short as the headline, stating the firing had taken place and the three bullets had all missed their mark. Clyde was contemptuous. "How could you miss a target that big?" he asked. "Ignoramuses! Stupidest thing I ever heard. Let me have that gun -- I could hit it."

In August of 1961, he turned fifty, yet he felt more like he slammed into fifty, or even that it overtook him, and he was not happy about it. Eve would chuckle and shake her head in amusement as she recounted that morning when Clyde awoke, and sat on edge of bed saying over and again, lowly and slowly, "I'm 50 years old," then putting on his trousers, repeating the words, and staggering into the kitchen for his first cup of coffee, still saying in a doomsday tone of voice, "I can't believe I'm 50 years old."

"It was hard on him," Eve said.

Clyde loved watching sports on TV, and liked to recall a time in the old days when things were different, when you tuned in the radio and sat around with others, leaning in close to hear a baseball game, or better yet, a prizefight. Clyde could picture it all in his mind: Gene Tunney, Jack Dempsey, Joe Louis, every blow delivered, and where it landed, and he would duck and parry the blows while he talked.

He loved watching professional football. His favorite team was the Dallas Cowboys, and his favorite player on the team was Bob Hays, an Olympic speed-burner who owned the record for the 100-meter dash, a man who got his mail addressed simply to *the world's fastest human.* And once during a game, after Bob Hays ran back a kick for a 96-yard touchdown, Clyde jumped up out of his easy chair and shouted, "I *love* Bob Hays -- I don't care *what* color he is[9]," bringing looks of surprise and consternation to everyone else in the room.

On another occasion, Clyde's reaction was not one of love and admiration after being deprived of watching his Cowboys. The town of Sanderson, lying at the bottom of a valley, had never had good TV reception until the early 60s during which time the city had a TV tower built atop one of the hills. A local person whose last name was Nance operated the tower in his spare time. Sometimes reception would weaken and Mr. Nance would get calls on the telephone to "fix" it. He would drive to the cabin at the bottom of the tower and do what he could, sometimes successfully, sometimes not. Once, while Clyde was watching the Cowboys play and the game had gotten very suspenseful, the outcome up for grabs, just as the quarterback, Don Meredith, was getting ready to launch a Hail Mary pass in Sudden Death overtime, the monitor turned into wiggly lines and screeching white noise -- no picture, no audio. Clyde walked over to the phone, picked it up and dialed a number he knew by heart. When the person on the other end of the phone answered, Clyde said, "Coon, you S.O.B![10]" and hung up. Then he walked outside and looked for things to do.

Like his father before him, Clyde had joined the Masons and was a dedicated member of the Masonic Lodge in Sanderson. Of a sudden, in 1967, he turned in serious pursuit of attaining his 32nd Degree – the second highest degree attainable in the Masonic Order. He and John Lewis went into it together, and doing so entailed long and frequent trips to El Paso. But sometimes Clyde would drive alone. On one such trip, he picked up four adolescent Blacks and took them to their destination near El Paso. He was tickled later that the four of them could all fit in the front seat of his Scout. He told them he was lonely for someone to talk to on the long drive. They discussed one of Clyde's favorite topics, which was Bob Hayes.

On another trip, he came across a young hitchhiker who, judging from the Union Jack he had sewn to his backpack, was British. Clyde had made no secret of his dislike for the British, claiming they talked in a silly, affected way, or that they lifted their little finger when they drank tea (his own father did the same), or that they drank tea at all, which was, for some reason Clyde never fully explained, unacceptable. Yet he found himself lonely on the road again, and pulled to a stop to give the Brit a lift.

As with the four Blacks, his former prejudices seemed to vanish on meeting the person, and he took an instant liking to the young man who called himself

---

[9] Paraphrased, *author*
[10] Paraphrased, *author*

Robin. Yes, he was from England, he said, and yes, he was British, and he was going to El Paso. He even admitted to preferring tea to coffee. As if he had discovered a long lost relative, Clyde took Robin everywhere with him. He detoured Robin from his original destination of El Paso. He paid his meals and lodging and truly enjoyed the young man's company. Their conversation stemmed mostly from subject matter dictated by Clyde: they talked about his background; coming up in Southwest Texas; working from Del Rio to Sanderson to Marathon, Marfa and the Chisos Mountains; the joys of flying; and things American, especially Bob Hayes and the Dallas Cowboys. And Robin would often convert Clyde's language into proper English, making Clyde howl with laughter to hear his prose given such elegance.

"The Dallas Cowboys are a *terrible* football team," Clyde emoted, emphatically drawing out the word to give it more meaning.

"In consideration for the pride you seem to feel for these Cowboys," interjected Robin, "I don't think you mean they're so much a poorly performing team as a *formidable* one." And on went their conversations.

When Robin had to return to England, Clyde admonished him he expected a written post card – and that if he didn't get one, he was going to go to England and hunt Robin down. Several weeks later, Clyde received his post card. He proudly carried it with him for a while and read from it aloud, until he lost it.

The flying bug, possibly before his daughter Beverly's marriage, bit Clyde early – perhaps as early as the two of them attempting to construct a gasoline-powered model airplane from a kit. It was built entirely out of tissue paper stretched over segments of balsa wood. To start the engine took a great deal of patience. Clyde and Beverly would take turns turning the propeller until the engine sputtered to life. Then they would release the airplane from a flat surface and watch it taxi and go airborne and promptly crash. Clyde would repair the broken wings -- a process that took days -- and then he and Beverly would fly it again. After it broke so many times he let the project go by the wayside.

Beverly married and took as a husband a career airman in the service. David owned a Piper Cub, loved to fly, and took every member of the family up for a ride at one time or another. Clyde flew with him, watched him maneuver, experienced the exhilaration of the freedom of flight, and was soon signed up for lessons to become a pilot. With a single-mindedness of purpose that had become expected of him, Clyde sought more than to learn the practice of flying, he "attacked" it; he absorbed and devoured it. And in short time, he was making his way from his latest flying lesson grinning, proudly displaying the clipped tail of his shirt as he walked, saying, "I got my wings." He had mastered his lessons and had passed all the required tests, including solo flight, and although Clyde was aware of what was about to happen, he welcomed the instructor sneaking up behind him and in the spirit of tradition, sawing off his shirt tail with a pocket knife. "Congratulations!" he had told Clyde, and that had been one of the proudest moments of his life, being officially admitted into the brotherhood of pilots.

Clyde was able to purchase a 1949 Piper Aeronca Chief. He kept it parked in a makeshift hangar on a graded strip of land on the Deaton ranch just west of town. He would come in from work on the railroad, and if there was enough daylight left, take the Aeronca for a spin. He flew it over the area in and around Sanderson, flew over the sparse traffic in the town and "buzzed" or wagged his wings at the cars of the people he recognized, seeing himself emulating the heroes of the Golden Age of Flight of whose exploits and derring-do he had read about over and again: stunt pilots and barnstormers like the great Wiley Post. In a tip of the hat to those heroes, he learned how to "short stop" a plane, or how to avoid the long descent onto a runway for a landing -- the way he had been taught -- idling his engine, rapidly losing altitude, and practically dropping in place on the tarmac before revving the engine again. It was a risky practice not without consequences. He had a couple of minor accidents. And he told the people around him that any crash he could walk away from was a "good crash."

Once, he had such a crash when his Aeronca Chief was caught in a crosswind and he was thrown against a guy-wire, shearing off the right wing. Both he and the plane were grounded until he could find a way to fix the wing. New wings were very expensive; the labor and cost of repairing the plane would be devastating to Clyde. He would fix it himself. He knew nothing about fixing airplanes or reattaching wings, but Clyde was convinced he could learn. While the plane sat wingless in the hangar on the west side of town, Clyde studied wing repair. He read; he talked to old-timers and airplane mechanics, and he took notes.

In order to repair his plane, he often had to drive great distances, forced to travel as far as Castroville for parts. Only years after he successfully repaired the wing and had it pass inspection with "flying colors," did he admit to Eve that on one of his long drives he had grown sleepy, remembering just before he nodded off, a highway sign indicating a certain town was 43 miles away, then suddenly awaking and seeing a new sign listing the same town as now 36 miles distant, startled he had driven seven miles in his sleep.

Flying, he felt, reinvigorated him, made him feel young again; after hearing that he drove in his sleep, Eve feared that on the ground, at least, he was growing old.

Then, one evening at the dinner table, apropos of nothing at all, when there was a lull in the conversation, Clyde said, "I know how I'm going to die."

Everyone looked up. He was rubbing the edge of his left ear. "I'm going to die of cancer," he said with absolute certainty. While the room remained quiet, Clyde went on to explain that he had had radium treatments on his ear and that the "bad place" didn't go away. He left the conclusion up to them. It was news to most at the table that he had undergone radium treatments at all, and it took a while for them to digest the information.

After a pause, he resumed eating. The rest of the table did as well. No word was spoken for the rest of the meal.

In 1967, Clyde and four other men the area, Barry Pendleton, Dee Carroll, Harvey Rogers and Horace Fletcher, pooled their resources and formed a flying club. Each member was to come up with a share of $2,500 so they could buy a new plane. It was a beauty: a powerful and fast 1967 four-seater Piper Comanche.

One of the objectives of the club was to provide assistance to the Civil Air Patrol, especially during search and rescue operations. During the following year, the club was involved in a few searches, but none successful.

In late June 1968, a plane flying from Odessa to Louisiana was lost with no trace. The CAP put out a call to all CAP members, of which the Sanderson flying club was one, to search for the lost plane. The Sanderson club joined similar clubs from Ft. Stockton and Odessa to cover the western leg of the search path.

Because of Clyde's railroad work schedule, he got only one opportunity to search. His flight log indicates he flew four hours round trip solo in the Comanche to Junction, Texas on July 7 to look for the lost plane. He did not find it. His next opportunity would be Saturday, July 13 after he returned from his trip to Valentine. Dee Carroll would go with him as co-pilot. Since it would be on a Saturday, his son Jack could go with them. Jack asked to take his friend Walter Shoemaker with him and Clyde agreed. Clyde and Dee also decided that Dee would fly so that he could gain more flying experience.

The fog, only patchy at first, and then more and more dense as they approached the Dryden airport, appearing at first in only the low-lying areas along the highway, and finally as pea soup, seemed to have slowly put strangle hold on the whole search and rescue operation, and any possibility of getting into the air that morning. When they arrived at the airport sometime before 6 am, visibility was zero.

All of them having emerged from the vehicle, standing on the tarmac in front of the headlights, able to see each other only as shadows, and nothing beyond, were forced to reassess their predicament. The prevailing viewpoint was that they had to leave now, no waiting. But what about the fog? "We'll get up out of if, and then we'll be home free." They would leave as planned.

Clyde had told Eve that he intended for Dee to fly, but no one knows who the pilot was that morning. There was no entry in the flight log for July 13th. At any rate, Clyde was not afraid of any situation. He believed in himself. He had braved the elements (with a small amount of luck) so many times before. He had carried grown men on his back up steep cliffs out of a rain-swollen Rio Grande, as well as surviving -- no, *overcoming* -- countless dangerous situations in the jungles of Mexico and the stormy waters of the Gulf of Mexico.

And even though he had flown instrument only on level flight, he felt he knew enough about instrument flying that he could maneuver the plane. It would be a rising banking turn to the left, up until he broke out of the fog. With a furtive glance at the dim runway lights to the left and to the right, the pilot pondered briefly, then pressed in the throttle to the roar of the engine and lifted off the end of Runway 13 into the blackness.

No one knows what happened after that, how the plane lifted off the tarmac only to nose-dive into an open field a few minutes and mere miles away. A railway crew working near the airport reported they heard a plane fly overhead at about 6 am. A Mexican man in the ranch house near where the crash occurred reported he had heard an explosion but had not gone to investigate it. The devastation was complete; there were no survivors.

Following the closed casket funerals, there was an investigation. The NTSB, coldly indifferent and analytical as ever, presented its findings:

> On 7/13/68, at 0600, Piper PA-28, registration N9092W, involved in a search and rescue operation, went into an uncontrolled descent near Dryden, Texas. There was fire after impact. Probable causes were:
>
> 1. Pilot in Command (PIC) attempted operation beyond experience/ability level
> 2. PIC continued VFR flight into adverse weather conditions
> 3. PIC suffered spatial disorientation
> 4. Low cloud ceiling, presence of fog.

Recovery date 7/15/68. Non-instrument-rated flight crew. Pilot in Command age 56, 200 lbs. 30 hours in type flying time, not instrument rated.

- Visibility at accident site: zero
- obstructions to vision at accident site: fog
- wind direction: 120 degrees
- type of weather conditions: IFR
- ceiling at accident site: 0
- precipitation at accident site: none
- temperature: 76F
- wind velocity: 8 knots
- type of flight plan: NONE.

However, in the Supreme Court of Texas case of *Shoemaker v. Estate of Whistler (July 10, 1974)*, some disagreement was found with the NTSB findings:

> "…it cannot be determined which of the joint owners, Carroll or Whistler, was the command pilot of the airplane at the times in question; for purposes of decision, we assume that Whistler was not."
>
> And further, "…Under the assumption we have been required to indulge, i. e., that Carroll and not Whistler was actually piloting the airplane at the times in question, Whistler could not have been expected to forcibly take the controls away from Carroll while in flight for the purpose of preventing the airplane from being flown into weather conditions requiring an instrument-rated pilot. For aught that appears from this record, such conditions may have developed after take-off and at a time when Whistler could not have been expected to take affirmative action, or would have had opportunity to do so."

And so the mystery of the crash continued to perpetuate itself. Good weather, bad weather; this pilot or that. The debris from the crash would lie on the open field basically unmolested, past the 1974 case and beyond, for another forty years.

# Chapter 27: Summing Up

According to NTSB records, of the 33 small aircraft crashes that occurred in the United States on July 13, 1968, only one resulted in fatality: Piper PA-28, Registration N902W, or what was termed the Flight of the Cherokee.

After the deaths of Clyde, Jack, Walter and Dee, flying in Sanderson died as well. Few had any stomach for it. Several years later, Barry Pendleton bought another plane and he continued to fly.

---

The impact of that flight found expression in sundry ways.

Eve received an unexpected sympathy card after the funerals. It was from Clyde's girlfriend from Depression-Era California. It was a colorful, flower-embossed card with a smoothly-flowing cursive note at the end saying, "It is fitting that Clyde should have died trying to help someone else." It was signed *Dorothy.*

Eve commented that it was nice, and put it aside.

She passed away four years later; both she and Clyde died at the same age, just before their 57$^{th}$ birthdays.

---

Two weeks before the crash, Zena had a vague, prophetic dream about darkness, disappearance, a bottomless cave, and childhood innocence. In her dream, which she didn't divulge until after the crash had occurred, she was presented with a choice of who would enter the cave, she or Clyde. She chose Clyde, regretting her words almost immediately.

The same year as his death she wrote a long poem titled *Saturday's Child,* chronicling her brother and his marvelous achievements from the Saturday of his birth to the Saturday of his demise.

---

Dotty penned a short piece titled *Vignettes,* about her father, the one called "1968" particularly revealing.

> Daddy was a man who could do anything. We kids all knew it from the time we were little. From a broken doll to a flat on our bikes, major appliances to model airplanes, he was the one we could go to for any repair. He could play a guitar, fix a windmill, make a car work, build a

house. The list goes on. He worked for the railroad, which took his time while there, but he brought no work home. As a result, he was able to pursue his hobbies during his off-hours, and he had many hobbies.

As his kids were getting grown up, the hobby he started pursuing was flying an airplane. I had joined the Navy in 1962 and he only had his wife and three sons left at home. In March 1964 he started taking flying lessons. He drove to Alpine, a town about 85 miles away, for flight lessons, about one every two weeks, while he shopped for an airplane. He had been at it for about 3 months when he found an old used airplane, an Aeronca Chief of 1941. He bought it and continued to take his lessons.

Daddy then towed the airplane to Alpine for a safety inspection and it was discovered that a wing had to be repaired. He decided that he could do the repairs more cheaply than paying for them done. Each step of that repair had to be approved by a professional organization, though, and none were in our town of Sanderson. He found someone he could take the detached wing to for inspections in Alpine. So he first stripped off the cover on the wing, and did the repair on the framework.

After he would repair the framework, he would tow the wing to Alpine, get approval on that step (or sometimes was told what he needed to do instead of what he had done), and tow the wing back home to start the next step. I don't know how many trips he made to get that wing flight-worthy and re-attached to the body, or how many hours he spent on the details of each set of repairs, but it was a bunch. Meanwhile, he continued to take the flight lessons, and finally he got the wing professionally recovered, passed a safety inspection on his airplane and a got a license to fly it in about April of 1965.

And fly it he did.

In mid-1964 his oldest son Louis had graduated from high school and joined the Navy. By mid-1966 Terry also graduated from high school and I had gotten out of the Navy. Terry and I then went to the same college in El Paso that fall. With only one son left at home Dad had lots more free time and a bit more money. By the fall of 1967 he got a private license, and, since the Aeronca was a two-seater, now he could legally take other people along on his journeys if he wanted. When he had a long trip to take, he would plot out his course and take his airplane for the trip.

Soon there came a request for a chapter of the Civil Air Patrol (CAP) to be started in Terrell County. There were frequent incidents of missing private (and sometimes commercial) airplanes, and the expanse across Terrell County and the adjoining counties in and near the Chihuahua Desert was vast. Daddy and several other pilots in the county did establish a CAP, probably in late 1967 or early 1968.

When an airplane was reported missing and it was suspected that it might have flown over Terrell County, the call went out for the CAP pilots to search for it. At first it was all done by the local pilots in their private airplanes, but soon several pilots went in together and purchased an airplane for the searches. This was a Piper Cherokee four-seater and pretty new with all the bells and whistles. It was kept at the airport in Dryden, about 20 miles from Sanderson.

By that March 1968, Louis had gotten out of the Navy and joined Terry and me in El Paso.

I came home for Easter break from college in April, 1968. I had not seen the new airplane, so it was a treat for me to get a chance to look it over. After Daddy and I took off from the airport at Sanderson in the Aeronca around 5 p.m., he told me on the 20-minute flight to Dryden that his airplane (the Aeronca) had no lights and the Sanderson runway had no landing lights. Dad had taken a course in IFR (Instrument Flight Rating) so that he was certified to fly in conditions where he could not see, like fog or rain, by using the instruments on his flight panel. But with no lights, we would have to get home before sunset at about 6:30 so he could see to land the airplane. That meant that we needed to leave the Dryden airport no later than 6:10, and probably 6:00 p.m. would be better.

We landed safely in Dryden's airport, and, as luck would have it, there were some other pilots there at the same time. Daddy struck up a conversation with them while I looked over the beautiful new "bird". And Dad was still talking to them when I had finished looking at it. A quick glance at my watch told me what the fading light in the sky was reinforcing. It was 6 p.m. and time for us to depart. I tugged on Daddy's sleeve, said we needed to go and ... he waved me away while he continued talking! I waited a few minutes, tugged again, with similar results. This was some important conversation, I guessed. A few more minutes, another attempt, still no movement. Finally at about 6:15, Daddy paid attention at last, looked at his watch and said, "We better git".

We climbed into the Aeronca, taxied out and took off. The light was really fading now. On the flight back to Sanderson, the shadows of the hills and trees grew longer and longer in the dimming light. Daddy explained to me that one of the problems with the runway in Sanderson (in addition to no landing lights) was that the runway was short, so the pilots needed to keep the airplane at flight speed at the beginning of it, but at a full stop (of course) at the end, which was tricky. Another problem was that the runway was surrounded by hills, so it was difficult to come in at a proper angle under proper speed - too much speed and you might be in a dive and have difficulty pulling out. Daddy's solution to the problem had been to get above the end of the runway and cut the engine! That way he could drift from side to side while the airplane descended, then at the proper elevation (pretty close to the ground), he would turn the engine on (hopefully), rev the engine to the proper speed and land under power. This did not sound so bad when attempted in daylight - Daddy could do most anything, as I have said before.

But this was not a daylight landing! There were no runway lights, no exterior airplane lights, and, now I realized, no interior lights! "I told you so," I said to myself, thinking about the earlier sleeve tugging.

Daddy fortunately had some matches, and as the sun eased down into the west, he asked me to strike a match so he could check his altitude and other readings. "I told you so," I thought again.

Soon I was lighting a match, holding it to the altimeter and speed indicator until it burned my fingers, putting it out and striking another. "I told you so!" became my under-my-breath mantra. But as we neared the Sanderson Airport, I realized I would rather die than tell my dad, "I told you so!" and with that realization, I became just his match-holder and came to a place of peace. Perhaps I would die, but I would not be disrespectful.

At the Sanderson Airport, the hills blocked any available light. We flew over them, lined up with what the compass told us was the proper direction, and Daddy cut the engine. We drifted left, then right, and then left again. The little match shone on the altimeter as he watched the gauge drop. A new match showed it was time to drift right again, then left to center the plane over the runway. Daddy turned the key, and the engine thankfully started right up. He powered up the engine and landed pretty well for doing it in the dark!

I have often thought about this adventure with my dad. He and my brother and two other people died in the CAP plane we had visited, just a few short months later. They took off in a heavy fog and crash-landed a few miles away. I have wondered if Daddy was the pilot. No flight plan

> was filed, so no one knows if it was he or the other pilot aboard who flew it. I have wondered if Daddy took a similar chance, taking off in a fog with zero visibility. Or if Dad thought he could help teach the other pilot how to fly in IFR conditions, since he (the other pilot) was not rated to do so. Maybe I'll ask him someday when we are reunited.

---

On the 45th anniversary of the plane crash, the Whistler children felt drawn to Sanderson to visit the crash site and to pay homage to Clyde and Jack. Louis and Terry had been to the site soon after the wreckage was recovered; they had forced themselves past officials who told them not to go in. Although the dead had been removed from the site, the two brothers had been witness to the devastation. They had seen parts of the instrument panel scattered over the field, the plane's clock half-buried in the ground, the hands frozen at 6:08; and they had seen Clyde's boots, all of which they had left behind. The other members of the Whistler family had never been to the site. Now they wanted, in all respect, to go back to it, but such was not to be. The family members stood at the gates to the ranch where the accident occurred, unable to go in because contact was not established with the rancher who owned the property.

However, the following year, Louis was successful in contacting the rancher and the Whistler and extended family was granted permission to visit the site. The mission was the same as on the first attempt. Louis recounted it later:

> I, Terry, Kathy, Dot, Brad, Beverly, and Anna met at the VFW Hall in Sanderson for breakfast at 6:30 AM Saturday, August 30. After breakfast, we drove to the ranch across from the airport at Dryden. The gates were open as Mike said they would be, and we met Mike in front of the ranch house. He said that he had this property for 17 years and that when he took it over, they did not tell him there had been a plane crash there more than 45 years ago. He found debris from the wreckage and figured out that it was from a plane. Because there had been no large plane parts, they thought the plane had exploded in midair. We told him that searchers had recovered all the major plane parts 46 years ago.
>
> Mike said that for 17 years he has been running deer hunters. He told everyone about the debris and said they could look at it. But out of respect for the dead and the possibility that someone might come back, he had told everyone to leave everything there. He said that his son recovered a watch and brought it to the house, but it was a long time ago, and he did not know where it was.

Mike said that we could drive our cars close. We had a car, a small pickup, and my large diesel Silverado. We drove near the site that Mike called the "Plane Crash Deer Feeder". We stopped near the blind on a shallow embankment and he pointed to the deer feeder further down the hill. He said it was rough, and we probably could not drive the cars. Mike told us that as relatives, we could take anything we found. Mike told us the debris field started about 20-30 feet from the feeder. Mike returned to the ranch house.

So, we all got into the diesel truck and drove down the hill to the feeder. (It was the same hill I remember walking down to the plane crash 46 years ago.) I left the truck running so that we could have an air conditioner if we needed it. We all fanned out and found the debris field after about a 20 minute search just to the north of the feeder. There were lots of small plane fiberglass parts. We found a tachometer, the internals for an altimeter, the chain drive for the flaps, a motor mount, a master key, the remains of a pocketknife, and we found the remains of Dad's boots.

We surveyed the debris field and it expanded in a cone shape starting about 40 feet north of the feeder. The field stretched for about 150 yards to the north and then stopped. We did not find the place where the engine ended up. Based on the shape of the debris field and on the location of dad's shoes, we located where the plane crash must have occurred. There was not a hole but there was a lot of soft ground there. This was not too far from the bottom of the hill, and it was reasonable that rain washing down the hill had filled in the hole during the past 46 years.

Dot burnt some incense at the crash location, and we stood around the place where the plane hit, holding hands while Dot recited a prayer for Dad, Jack, and the other departed.

---

Deer, jackrabbits, and coyotes had crisscrossed the area; hunters had walked there; 46 summers had scorched the earth; and the debris stayed. Looking out over it all, under a morning sun that was already growing oppressive, superimposing past memories over what lay before him now, Louis added further comment:

…thinking of the scope of time those shoes waited on the plains for us to return. The remaining children went through marriages, divorces, re-marriages, children birthed - raised to adults - sent to college, grand children born, and even some great grandchildren birthed. There were college careers completed, employment, careers begun and completed. And, yet those shoes waited silently on the plains through all of that - 46 years. What a span of time.

Talk about a time machine. Touching those shoes took me back to the day we first saw them, examined them and left them at the spot. To me, it is almost as if it were yesterday. Those shoes are the true testament to the legacy left behind by Dad and Jack. They will live on in my mind frozen in time.

And so they do, for us all.

END

*Forty-six years after the crash. Artifacts from an open field near Dryden, Texas. July 2014.*

# Appendix 1

Lyrics to *Bangum,* a song dating back to King Arthur's Court in the Thirteenth Century

There is a wild boar in these woods
Dillo-day, dillo-day
There is a wild boar in these woods
Dillo-day down
There is a wild boar in these woods
He kills young men and he drinks their blood.
Come away, cuddle down
Killo-quay-quan

Bangum made a wooden knife
Dillo-day, dillo-day
Bangum made a wooden knife
Dillo-day down
Bangum made a wooden knife
He swore he'd take that wild boar's life.
Come away, cuddle down
Killo-quay-quan

Bangum rode to the wild boar's den
Dillo-day, dillo-day
Bangum rode to the wild boar's den
Dillo-day down
Bangum rode to the wild boar's den
There lay the bones of a hundred men.
Come away, cuddle down
Killo-quay-quan

He put his horn up to his mouth
Dillo-day, dillo-day
He put his horn up to his mouth
Dillo-day down

He put his horn up to his mouth
He blew it north, east, west and south.
Come away, cuddle down
Killo-quay-quan

Out come that wild boar running dash
Dillo-day, dillo-day
Out come that wild boar running dash
Dillo-day down
Out come that wild boar running dash
He cut his way through oak and ash.
Come away, cuddle down
Killo-quay-quan

They fought for hours on the plain
Dillo-day, dillo-day
They fought for hours on the plain
Dillo-day down
They fought for hours on the plain
At last that wild boar he was slain.
Come away, cuddle down
Killo-quay-quan

Lyrics to *Oh, Don't You Believe it*

When I was a young man about twenty
I thought that I knew everything
Till I met a man on the corner
who sold me a beautiful ring.
He whispered, "Young, man, it's a bargain,
This gold is the finest you've seen."
I thought that it must be from Ireland
when it turned my finger green.

Oh don't you believe it
I don't give a darn what they say
This whole world is chuck full of liars
and a new one is born every day.

My old man said I was a dumbbell.
I left the house in a huff.
He said, "If you never come back here,
that will be soon enough."
I stayed a few weeks with the neighbors.
I thought he would quickly repent.
But when I wrote him a letter,
this is the message he sent -

Oh, don't you believe it.
This comes from all of the folks.
If you think we're pining to see you,
Think up some more funny jokes.

I heard there was gold in Alaska,
I made a dash right away
If there's any gold in them gosh darn hills,
as fur's I'm concerned it can stay,
I bought me a pick and a shovel,
I worked night and day without rest,
but all that I got for my trouble,
was a darn good cold in the chest.

Oh, don't you believe it
I thought I was smart as a fox
but I dug a hole clear to China,
and never found nothing but rocks

I thought I'd be safe in the Army,
and never work anymore,
but I had just hardly got settled,
when somebody started a war.
They rushed me right up to the trenches,

the captain wished all of us luck.
Then he beat it right back to Paris.
I hope he got hit with a truck

Oh, don't you believe it.
They said what a hero I'd be.
I said you guys keep all your medals
and give me my Li-ber-ty.

www.ingramcontent.com/pod-product-compliance
Ingram Content Group UK Ltd.
Pitfield, Milton Keynes, MK11 3LW, UK
UKHW041942190726
13854UKWH00004B/1748

9 781312 730052